JOE DIEFFENBACHER

Joe Dieffenbacher is an author and actor known for his theatre, circus and cabaret performances under the name nakupelle.

He was Physical Comedy Director for *The Taming of the Shrew* at Shakespeare's Globe, London, and Regent's Park Open Air Theatre's production of *Oliver!* He worked as Physical Theatre Director for *Woman and Scarecrow* at the Royal Academy of Dramatic Art, London, and served as Circus Skills Director for the Scottish National Opera's *Ariadne auf Naxos*. He was playwright, prop designer and director for *Servant of Two Masters* at Coastal Carolina University, and for numerous productions with the Dell'Arte Players, California.

As director of Clown Conservatory at the Circus Center, San Francisco, he developed an extensive pedagogy combining Clown, Circus, Theatre, Slapstick and Commedia. His work was featured on ABC News: Clown School: Day in the Life, and part of the documentary, *Bizarre: A Circus Story*.

Joe served as lead instructor for Clown, Physical Theatre, Mask Performance and Slapstick at Dell'Arte International, and has been a guest teacher at the Belfast Community Circus, Teater Studion in Stockholm, Wuqiao International Circus Festival, Shijiazhuang, China, and the American Conservatory Theater in San Francisco. He has worked with solo artists and ensembles all over the world, developing original material for theatre, circus, cabaret, dance theatre and outdoor spectacles.

As a clown and physical comedian, Joe has collaborated on six productions with British pop sensations Take That, co-created sequences for the Closing Ceremonies of the London 2012 Olympics and Paralympics, was a clown and elephant jumper with the Ringling Bros. and Barnum & Bailey Circus, and collaborated on shows for Disney in California and Florida. His own company, nakupelle, has been featured in theatre seasons, outdoor festivals, circuses and cabarets in Europe, Asia and North America.

www.joedieffenbacher.com

www.nakupelle.com

DRAMA GAMES is a series of books for teachers, workshop leaders and directors in need of new and dynamic activities when working with actors in education, workshop or rehearsal.

Also available in this series:

DRAMA GAMES FOR ACTORS
Thomasina Unsworth

**DRAMA GAMES
FOR CLASSROOMS AND WORKSHOPS**
Jessica Swale

DRAMA GAMES FOR DEVISING
Jessica Swale

**DRAMA GAMES
FOR EXPLORING SHAKESPEARE**
*Alanna Beeken and
Coram Shakespeare Schools Foundation*

DRAMA GAMES FOR REHEARSALS
Jessica Swale

**DRAMA GAMES
FOR THOSE WHO LIKE TO SAY NO**
Chris Johnston

DRAMA GAMES FOR YOUNG CHILDREN
Katherine Zachest

And more to follow…

The publisher welcomes suggestions for further titles in the series.

Joe Dieffenbacher

drama games

FOR CLOWNING AND PHYSICAL COMEDY

Foreword by John Wright

NICK HERN BOOKS
London
www.nickhernbooks.co.uk

A Nick Hern Book

DRAMA GAMES FOR CLOWNING
AND PHYSICAL COMEDY

First published in Great Britain in 2025
by Nick Hern Books Limited
The Glasshouse, 49a Goldhawk Road,
London W12 8QP

Copyright © 2025 Joe Dieffenbacher
Foreword copyright © 2025 John Wright

Joe Dieffenbacher has asserted his moral right
to be identified as the author of this work

Designed and typeset by Nick Hern Books, London
Printed and bound in Great Britain by
SRP Ltd, Exeter

A CIP catalogue record for this book
is available from the British Library

ISBN 978 1 84842 901 7

www.nickhernbooks.co.uk/environmental-policy

Nick Hern Books' authorised representative in the EU is
Easy Access System Europe – Mustamäe tee 50, 10621 Tallinn, Estonia
email gpsr.requests@easproject.com

*For Will Chamberlain
of the Belfast Community Circus*

*Clown, Mover and Shaker,
Friend and Inspiration*

John Wright is an award-winning international teacher and theatre-maker. He co-founded Trestle Theatre Company in 1980 and Told by an Idiot in 1993. He has worked on a string of productions and projects extending over three decades in Europe, Scandinavia, Asia and the UK, where his work has been seen at the National Theatre, the RSC, the Royal Court, the Almeida and the Royal Opera House.

He was granted a Greater London Arts Award for his contribution to professional training; and his belief that teaching is the greatest source of learning has enabled his ideas to be shaped and moulded by generations of students. He pioneered the teaching of Clown at university level and was one of the first people in the country to offer courses in devising.

He is the author of two books, *Why Is That So Funny?: A Practical Exploration of Physical Comedy* and *Playing the Mask: Acting Without Bullshit*, both published by Nick Hern Books.

FOREWORD

In this highly practical compendium, Joe Dieffenbacher offers a rich collection of games designed to reveal and enhance the skills of play, clowning and physical comedy.

Some of his games are immediate and self-explanatory, and inspire playfulness without further elaboration. *Snatch Tail* is a typical example. It's a simple interaction game that can be played in many different ways, depending on the needs of the group. You can play it with aggression, skill, mindless generosity, abject terror or a cunning combination of all these things. It's as simple as *Tag*, you might think; but *Snatch Tail* is a game that gives you much more to do and offers far greater opportunities to engage the audience's attention and make them laugh than *Tag* is ever likely to do.

Another of Joe's games that stands out for me is *Orkestra*, which has immense potential for inspiring the chaos, surprise, nonsense and bafflement of Clown. This is the game of five people trying to convince us that they can sing a song they all know, with the many harmonies that go with it, when in reality they don't have a song to sing and know very little about music. This game offers a multitude of possibilities for all the complexities of suspense, delight, distress, anarchy and relief. It's an inspiring invitation to clown-play.

Both of these games are simple enough to require little explanation. They offer participants so much to play with, and immense scope for fun and clowning – and Joe gives us some eighty games like this in this book. The first few are there to build the skills of the group and establish the status of 'playing the game'. They celebrate the task of doing something simply for the fun of it, as opposed to playing a dramatic encounter credibly. Other groups of games explore solo play and group play. His vigorous complicity games are a reminder that some of the most challenging spontaneity happens at speed. There are more collaborative games constructed from simple dramatic structures that can be applied in many ways, while other games here will inspire brilliant physical comedy. There are innumerable variations on familiar themes and different approaches to the big questions inherent in making comedy.

With so many games to play and to enjoy, Joe's collection is a constant reminder that games aren't remotely real. A game is something you play to deliberately have an effect on others. They pinpoint responses and ideas that can be repeated, revised and messed about with to suit any particular group of players.

Play comes in many forms, and Joe's games inspire fun, experiment and discovery. It's the potential for engagement and fun that wins our respect for a game. We remember the games we enjoy. The best games can be left to stand for themselves, and in this book all the thoughts, feelings and justifications behind the games are cut back to a satisfying minimum. I rarely read books of theatre games, but Joe Dieffenbacher has made me think again.

There are eighty games in this book: eighty opportunities to capture a mood, provoke a response and excite creativity. They are a gift.
I wish I'd had this book a couple of decades ago.

John Wright
London, 2025

CONTENTS

Foreword by John Wright — vii

Introduction — xiii

How to Use This Book — xv

Acknowledgements — xx

Part One: ENERGY
Building and strengthening the ensemble

1.	Name Games	4
2.	Aura	5
3.	Hands to Hands	6
4.	Lean On Me	8
5.	Human Springs	10
6.	Knot, Spiral, Pulse	11
7.	Awareness	12
8.	Breath and Movement	14
9.	Count Up, Count Down	16
10.	Ha-Ha-Ha! Wah-Wah-Wah…	18

Part Two: PLAY
Creating connections through physical play

11.	Let's Dance	24
12.	Alien, Cow, Lion	27
13.	Mouse, Cat, Dog, Horse, Eagle	28
14.	Clap It Round	30
15.	Chase and Tag	32
16.	Eyes Closed	34
17.	You–Me	36

| 18. | Game On | *38* |
| 19. | Buf Da | *40* |

Part Three: CURIOSITY
Encouraging listening as well as imaginative, improvised play

20.	Wide-Eyed	*46*
21.	Point of Focus	*48*
22.	Takes	*50*
23.	Chain Reaction	*53*
24.	Entrances and Exits	*54*
25.	The Audience: Hands	*56*
26.	The Eyes Have It: Choices	*58*

Part Four: COMPETITION
Using competition to develop ensemble play

27.	Ha-goo	*64*
28.	Fox and Squirrel	*66*
29.	Dragon's Jewels	*68*
30.	Snatch Tail	*70*
31.	Snatch the Prize	*72*

Part Five: COLLABORATION
Exploring the dynamics of collaborating (and collaborating while competing)

32.	Pressure Points	*78*
33.	Dance and Get Off the Floor	*79*
34.	Body Hide	*80*
35.	Snake Pit	*82*
36.	Orkestra	*84*
37.	Who Started It?	*86*

Part Six: PROVOCATION
Developing physical and mental flexibility with help from partners and the audience

38.	The Audience: Yay! Boo!	*90*
39.	Nice and Nasty	*91*
40.	The Provocateur	*92*

| 41. | In and Out – But Only Two | 94 |
| 42. | Pop Goes the Beastie | 96 |

Part Seven: COMPLICATION
Using restrictions, problems and accidents to generate material

43.	The Invaders	102
44.	Task and Time	104
45.	The Eyes Have It: The Trick	106
46.	The Variation	108
47.	Incoming!	110

Part Eight: IMPROPISATION
Using props to reveal thoughts, emotions, develop relationships and devise material

48.	Object Leads	114
49.	Props-Go-Round	115
50.	Properazzi	116
51.	Prop Offers	118

Part Nine: PHYSICALITY
Exploring and improving physical expressiveness

52.	Pass It Round	122
53.	Embodied Image	123
54.	Wind-Up, Stall, Repeat, Breathe	124
55.	Pick a Mask	126
56.	Physicalise a Phrase	128
57.	Party Animals	130

Part Ten: CLOWN SOLO
Developing a solo Player's skills and generating performance material

58.	Segmented	136
59.	The Set-Up and the Scene	138
60.	The Benign Dictator	140
61.	Shifty Solos	142
62.	Solo Variations: Atmospheres	144
63.	Seven Snapshots	148

Part Eleven: CLOWN DUO
Developing partner relationships and generating performance material for duos

64.	Walk Like Me	154
65.	Cane Connection	156
66.	Mirrors and Shadows	157
67.	Dogged	160
68.	The Solo Duet	162

Part Twelve: CLOWN TRIO
Exploring status and the dynamics of a trio

69.	Lookers	168
70.	Be Seated	170
71.	Three Coats, Three Hats and a Bench	172
72.	Props, People, Status	174
73.	Let Me Handle This	176
74.	Disadvantaged	178

Part Thirteen: CLOWN ENSEMBLE
Developing complicity, group improv, and ensemble storytelling skills

75.	Tableaux	186
76.	Machines and Slow-Motion Scenes	188
77.	Repel and Lookout	190
78.	The Journey	192
79.	The Preposterous Players	194
80.	The Escalating Party	196

Index of Games

Skills	200
Alphabetical List	204
Complete List	205

INTRODUCTION

There is nothing predictable about clowns. They don't act a certain way, they can't be confined to a single character, they aren't limited to a certain look. They thwart any attempt at explaining who they are, they won't be relegated to mere words.

So how do you teach something that resists being defined? How can you introduce it to students, ask them to consider it thoughtfully, while it dances around them, seemingly always out of reach?

Perhaps the best way to learn about clowning, then, is to join the dance: get up and move, relate, play.

I define play as a way of exploring and learning through active engagement with the world. Play as a way of creating connections and fostering relationships in order to deepen your understanding and expand your imaginations.

The main objective of all the games and exercises in this book is to develop the playful mind (and body) of each Player. It is this playful mind that begets the clown, for *a clown is a person always at play*, engaging physically, emotionally and mentally with everything around them. They play not only with physical, visible worlds, but hidden and imaginary worlds as well.

Clowning gets dressed up in different ways, has certain traditions and styles, but, at its core, it is a way of interacting with the world through play. This play is inspired by curiosity, which is piqued by a desire to reach out to the world and immerse yourself in it; the best clowning isn't narrowly focused on just getting laughs. This is one of the reasons why clowning is useful for anyone trying to encourage participation and creativity, individual invention, and ensemble exploration.

I've used these exercises with actors, improvisers, stand-up comedians, circus acts, musical-theatre actors, Renaissance players, cabaret artists, mask performers, Shakespearean actors, Commedia troupes, opera singers, at-risk youths and business executives. Some participants had known each other for months, others only met that morning. I've used them with tight ensembles that have collaborated for years, and with groups struggling to find a way to connect. They've been part of one-day workshops, seven-week intensives and four-year graduate programmes exploring physical-theatre styles. They're useful for groups wishing to use the insights of clowning to develop original work and to bring a new approach to existing plays. Many exercises will serve the entire ensemble, others are focused on solo, duo and trio work; these can be used to develop standalone routines and scenes, or to enhance duo and trio relationships within a larger, scripted play.

HOW TO USE THIS BOOK

Terminology

I refer to students as *the Players*, and the leader of the session as *the Guide*. There are *exercises* – which are focused on specific techniques or concepts – and *games* – which also teach specifics but in a more free-form way. I vary the use of he, she and they to describe the Players. In this Introduction, some things are directed to you, the reader (whether acting as the Guide or the Player).

Preparation at the start of some exercises will suggest ways to prepare the space or the Players for what the exercise will require. It will also address any safety issues. The word *Listening* in the *Skills* section at the end of the exercises refers not only to listening with the ears but with the entire body. This encourages not only an awareness of one's own body, but that of others around you.

I have structured this book so it starts small and goes big (in clown terms, minimum-to-MAXIMUM). It begins with two Players standing face to face and sensing each other's energy, learning to communicate on this most basic level. From there things expand: the Players begin to move with each other, they make contact, the playing gets more vigorous; ideas, emotions, movements and objects are tossed their way and they play with it all – while maintaining the awareness of the simple energy exchange experienced in the first exercises.

As the playing expands, it can get a little crazy, at times bewildering. But curiosity, engaging and relating are always emphasised. The Players will begin to delight in the hustle-bustle, wonder at the feeling of being overwhelmed by it all, and enjoy the opportunity to share this moving puzzle with others. Slowly they begin to see that the apparent madness in all this movement and play can be a method, a pathway to learning. The exercises in this book lead the Players towards comprehending this through *active participation*. They'll experience a greater connection to the group, a deeper understanding of how a clown responds to and shapes their world, and the expression of that world in performance.

Notes are clarifications or suggestions directed at the Guide to help them prepare the Players for a game or exercise. They can also be used to coach the Players as they explore.

The comments under *Side-coaching* give more information about the objectives of an exercise and suggest ways for the Players to get more out of it. They can be used by the Guide to enhance the teaching process, or by the Players who are exploring an exercise on their own (without it being led by the Guide).

The one facilitating the workshop acts as an outside eye, an adviser, the Guide. It is their job to explain the rules, and in the early stages of an exercise, remind the Players to stick to them. They're also the *Boss*, playing the role of the authority figure in the group. This is not stated outright. Will the Players realise that this is the game the Guide is also playing? When does it begin? Will the Players start not only to bend and break the rules, but playfully challenge the Boss's authority? When they catch on, they should toy with the tension between rebellious play and the structure demanded by the rules and the authority of the Boss. This tension is important in clowning. When this is understood and acted out, both the Players and the Guide realise and develop the game within the game.

Game Sources

These games come from a number of sources and have been developed, added to and refined by me over the course of many years, with students from all over the world, and many different performance styles. Some are drawn from books on children's games, others from actors or improvisers. I have modified them or created variations to serve some aspect of clowning and physical comedy. Some I invented to help teach things specific to clown or devising new material. I hope they will inspire you and you'll develop your own variations, invent new rules, then bend and break them to continue to expand the possibilities of your work and your play!

Preparation

All of the exercises involve some form of physical play, so make time at the beginning of each session to prepare the participants physically. Some of the exercises in this book can be used as warm-ups (especially those in the first half), but you may want to include basic cardio, stretching and vocal warm-ups as well.

The Players should wear clothing that is easy for them to move in but not too loose. Belts, bracelets, necklaces, earrings, etc. should be removed. The Players work barefoot or in their socks, but should have a pair of shoes handy, ones they can wear in the studio to protect their feet during some exercises. Costume elements can be added as the Players start developing ideas about a 'clown look', and when working on solo, duo and trio acts and scenes.

If you can get hold of gym mats – thick ones that Velcro together, not yoga mats – they will create a good surface for warm-ups and are useful for some games. Any props needed are listed at the bottom of each exercise.

Before beginning every session, check the space for any potential hazards: changes in floor levels, sharp corners, loose bits on the floor that might be tripped over, things on the walls that might fall off. Encourage the Players to do the same *every time* they enter the room (things may have changed since the last session). This process also gets them familiar with the space and may offer ideas on how to use the space during an exercise or in performance.

If you choose to jump ahead to the later sections in the book – **Clown Duos**, **Trios** and **Ensembles** (pages 151–97) – it's advisable to play a few games at the start of each session first to get the Players moving and engaging with each other (the **Skills** section at the back of the book – page 200 – describes which games are good for warm-ups and introductions).

Some exercises will dig deeper, demand more from the Players physically, mentally and emotionally. Stay sensitive to the progress of each participant; prepare them for things you think might challenge them, reminding them to keep safety at the forefront of their minds.

Some games will have more than one variation. Many of these were developed with Players who bent the rules, sought to turn the game to their advantage, or were confused by the rules and inadvertently invented new ones. Others grew out of the Players' mastery of a game and my desire to challenge them further. I encourage you to do the same and develop more variations. This is an important process, one that should be pointed out to the Players, as it mirrors the way clown acts and devised scenes are developed. Like a game, the Players start with a few ideas, a few rules. They decide on a basic scenario and begin to play, adhering to what they've decided on at the outset, and in the midst of their explorations, start to deviate, invent, go beyond what was decided and expand the possibilities of the scenario.

I usually don't teach traditional clown routines but instead, through the exercises and games, try to develop in the Players the *mind of a clown*, so they start to see the potential for play and physical comedy in any situation, and how to transform what they discover into performance material. I also want to improve the Players' ability to express themselves physically: all of the games make use of the body, encouraging the Players to find multiple ways to convey thoughts and emotions by how they use their faces, arms, hands, torsos, spines – even their feet!

This is why I use games for training: they get participants used to playing and connecting that to performing, so they carry the energy of play from the classroom to the stage. Their performance for an audience is treated as a game with rules that are meant to be obeyed, but open to alteration by both the Players and the audience. This approach encourages their participation: the Players invite their audience to join in and explore the game *with* them, and give the crowd licence – overtly and subtly – to suggest their own take on the rules (the script).

In terms of devising and developing original material, I find games useful in understanding how to use the authority established by the rules (and the Guide who defines what those rules are), to create a foil, a controller, an adversary. This is someone that the Players want to serve (do what they are told to do), but also want to go beyond to expand the possibilities of their play. Learning how to utilise and toy with this tension between open-ended play and sticking to the script is important for creating and plotting devised material, especially for clowning. Underneath the routine or scene you're playing, there is the structure established by the script (the rules). This is supported – but also challenged by – the dynamic, exuberant energy of the playful mind of the clown, and their desire to bend and break the rules to broaden the potential of a moment or scene in order to create connections between the scripted performance and the audience. As the performance unfolds and the story is revealed, the relationship between the audience, the Players and their performance is deepened and celebrated. The script – and the story it is telling – expands and manifests the greatest gift a live performance can give: a genuine, open, human connection between the Players and their audience.

ACKNOWLEDGEMENTS

I am deeply indebted to my students all over the world who have helped me develop and refine my craft, and shared their minds, bodies and hearts.

I am grateful to the institutions I have trained and taught at, thankful that they keep the fire burning. These spaces seek creativity and play in all its myriad forms, from the silly to the serious, the skilful to the mischievous. If there is a circus or theatre training space in your neighbourhood, please support it by taking classes, going to see their productions, and making donations of time and money.

To John O'Donovan and all those at Nick Hern Books who supported the publication of this book and gave me excellent advice.

To my parents – my biggest inspiration – and my brothers and sister – my first audience. I thank them for teaching me the fine art of slapstick (inadvertently), putting up with my early attempts at creating comedy, and for listening, laughing and inspiring me. The bond that we share is the same one I try to create with my students and my audience.

And my wife Minna who, after so many years together, still laughs at my jokes.

PART ONE

ENERGY

Building and strengthening the ensemble

I believe the clown is not a character but an energy, a way of creating and performing that is inspired by pure play; chaotic and rambunctious, subtle and still – and everything in between. What is this 'energy' that clowning embodies? How does a Player experience it to such a degree that they can channel it and share it with their partners and their audience?

It starts with their attention; the Players facing their partners, opening up to them, trying to connect with them on a level that is not visible nor easy to articulate; they engage with each other, learning to be present, available, responsive.

The Players thus begin a process of getting to know their partners on many levels: visual, physical, mental and emotional. They explore how they move together, how things change when they make contact, how they lead and follow. They learn each other's weaknesses and strengths; they don't judge or comment on anything they discover, they simply observe in order to get to know their partners in a way that eschews words and reaches for something deeper.

When the Players feel themselves in alignment with their partner and connected to the group, they experience an exchange of energy that expresses the solidarity that strong ensembles have; some call it complicity – it can feel like telepathy. As they develop and expand on this, it spreads outwards towards the audience. This is the pleasure – the excitement! – that is felt when watching strong ensembles. The group's energy connects with that of the audience, they feel part of the play, eager to go on a journey with the ensemble.

The following exercises begin this process, encouraging Players to get to know one another, to connect via the energy that is released when people focus on active play, listening with their bodies and all their senses.

Name Games

A good game to start with, giving the Players a chance to introduce themselves in a playful, physical way.

In-a-Circle Style: The Players stand in a circle. The Guide introduces herself (full name). The Player to her left introduces herself. Continue around the circle.

The Guide introduces herself again then styles to – physically presents/points to, with hands, arms, face and full-body pose – the Player to her left, who introduces herself and styles to the next person. Continue around the circle.

This time the Guide styles to the Player to her left and introduces her, e.g. 'This is Jennie!' Jennie bows and, as the rest of the group repeats her name, they cheer, applaud, give her a thumbs-up, etc. When this ends, Jennie styles to the next Player, introduces him and the group responds. Continue around the circle.

Mexican-Wave Name: The Players stand in a circle. The Guide starts by extending his arms overhead and when they peak, he says his first name, e.g. 'Joe!' As he brings his arms down, the Player to his left extends both arms in the air and when they peak, he repeats the name, 'Joe!' As he starts to bring his arms down the next Player in the circle lifts her arms repeating the name. This continues, creating a Mexican wave around the circle, with the name and the movement repeated by each Player.

When it gets back to the Guide, the Player to his left calls out his own name; the next Player to his left starts the Mexican wave again with this new name. Continue this pattern around the circle.

Skills
Introductions, Warm-Up

Aura

This exercise introduces the idea and the sensation of connecting with a partner by opening up to their energy.

The Players partner up and face each other, arm's length apart. They place their hands palm to palm (arms extended, elbows slightly bent). Once they have this point of contact, they close their eyes (keep them closed throughout the exercise) and focus on their hands, sensing the energy that passes between them via their palms.

When they feel they have a strong sensation of their partner's energy, they slowly draw their hands back until they are close to their own chest, keeping their palms out the whole time. They try to feel and focus on the energy radiating from their palms, like lines of electricity travelling from hand-to-hand.

Each Player turns in a circle in place three times. On the third turn, they stop, hands still up, and try to reconnect, palm to palm with their partner. They shouldn't open their eyes, reach out or grope in space, nor make sounds; they should concentrate on the energy emanating from their palms to find their partner and reconnect.

Skills
Collaboration, Duos, Introductions

Hands to Hands

A game for playing with physical give-and-take, leading and following.

Push Hands to Hands: The Players partner up. They press their hands together palm-to-palm and maintain this contact throughout the game. One Player is *Pusher*, the other *Pushed*.

Using only the contact between their hands, Pusher begins to push her partner around the room. Pushed toys with his level of resistance: sometimes he makes it hard to be moved, other times he lets himself be pushed, either by keeping his feet in place and moving just his arms, or letting his whole body be pushed around the room. The Guide gives a signal and they switch roles.

After partners have played both roles, they switch back and forth without any signal from the Guide: in the midst of the playing, Pushed suddenly decides to push back, Pusher letting herself be pushed. They explore the moments of transition induced by the switches: how long do they resist changing roles, how easily do they give in?

Push Parts: Pusher pushes different parts of their partner's body; Pushed explores how that affects those parts.

For example, pushing against an elbow might cause the rest of the arm to flap, push the head and it might move just from the neck up, or shift the entire body. Pusher plays with how different degrees of force affect their partner's body. The Guide gives a signal and they switch roles.

Note: The push is not aggressive; Pusher makes contact and then pushes, playing with the degree of force applied. It's a way of physically directing a partner through space or moving a part of their body. Think of it as a dance not a competition.

These explorations are great for clown partners: the interactions immediately reveal to the audience a relationship between the clowns that is both physical and visual. Comic play can develop by toying with contrasts: a strong push can lead to a small reaction, or a tap on the shoulder causes the clown to collapse to the floor.

Skills
Collaboration, Duos, Following, Leading, Warm-Up

4

ENERGY

Lean On Me

A trust game that has the Players supporting one another in playful ways.

Back to Back: The Players partner up. They stand back against back, leaning in to each other, giving each other a bit of their weight. Maintaining this back-to-back connection, partners move about the room, 'listening' to each other via their backs. They can both sit, or one Player can lift the other onto her back, or even go into a push-up position with the other lying on their back.

The Players explore ways of following or leading one another around the space, and all the possibilities of partner play and movement, while maintaining the back-to-back connection.

Body Part to Body Part: Same as above, but the connection point could be head-to-head, palm-to-palm, shoulder-to-shoulder, etc. Or mix palm-to-head, chest-to-shoulder, upper-back-to-forearm. The Players give each other weight and lean in to each other for support, as they explore movement possibilities *together*.

Touch Twister: The Players find a partner. They stand facing each other. The Guide calls out body parts. The Players touch these parts together; for example, the Guide calls 'Forehead-to-forehead!' and the Players touch their foreheads together. The Guide then calls 'Foot-to-knee!' and one Player touches his foot to the knee of his partner while maintaining the forehead-to-forehead connection. The partners work together to maintain their balance, but the only contact is what the Guide calls out (they don't hold each other's arms to stay upright).

The Guide continues to call out body parts until it's impossible for the Players to hold their positions (the Guide can also say, 'Stop doing foot-to-knee' if she wants to subtract an idea and try a different point of contact). The Guide calls the game to an end. The Players find new partners and the game begins again.

4

ENERGY

Note: Simple, playful, physical contact is vital to helping the Players loosen up, befriend one another, trust one another and, most importantly, break down barriers so they can openly play with one another, especially in the early stages of a class or a rehearsal. In clowning, physical interaction is crucial.

Skills
Collaboration, Duos, Introductions, Listening, Warm-Up

5

ENERGY

Human Springs

A good game for developing physical trust between two people, and learning to take risks with a partner.

The Players partner up and face each other about two metres apart. They stand with their bodies straight, feet together, arms out, extended straight in front of their bodies at chest height in the direction of their partner opposite them. Wrists are flexed so palms are open to partner's palms. Both the Players tip forward, bodies stiff as planks, and fall towards one another, reaching out and catching palm-to-palm (the four fingers of each hand wrap around the space between partner's index finger and thumb). They bend their arms, bringing their collar bones close together (like an upside-down V), dropping their head over their partner's shoulder. Working together, they extend their arms at the same time and push off, letting go of each other's hands so they stand up straight without shifting their feet or going off-balance (this works best when timed together, both the Players using equal force to push their partner upright). Once they can do this successfully, partners increase the distance. How far apart can they go and still push each other upright?

Side-coaching

- The Players should be reminded not to rush the push-off: they take a moment and breathe together before pushing, and work to be in sync, especially if they're mismatched (e.g. tall and less tall, strong and not as strong).

- As the distance increases, the Players must find just the right way to catch each other, lean in close, then push off, so they come out of the tilt at the same time, and neither Player loses their balance or shifts their feet. It's more subtle than it might first appear.

Skills
Collaboration, Duos, Introductions, Trust, Warm-Up

Knot, Spiral, Pulse

A series of games for ensemble-building and focusing the energy of the group.

Knot: The Players stand close together, both hands reaching into the centre. They grab hold of another Player's hands at random. Once all are holding two hands, the group works together to untangle the knot and spread out into a circle without letting go.

Spiral: Once they untie the knot, with the Players all facing the same direction, a Player on one end becomes the centre. He stays stationary. The Player on the other end pulls the group to spiral around the centre – still holding hands – until the entire group is wrapped snugly around the centre Player. To come out of it, the Player at the centre climbs through legs or under arms to the outside, leading the group out – *holding hands the entire time* – unwrapping until all are in a line again. Once complete, try wrapping around a new centre Player, or move on to the next variation.

Pulse: The Players now link hands to form a circle. The Guide starts a pulse by squeezing the hand of the Player to his right, who then squeezes the hand of the Player to her right and so on, sending the pulse/squeeze around the circle.

The Guide gets more than one pulse going in the same direction. The Guide gets another pulse going in the opposite direction.

The Guide sends a pulse left. The Players say 'Oh!' when someone squeezes their right hand. The Guide sends a pulse right. The Players say 'Ah!' when someone squeezes their left hand. Try multiple pulses in different directions.

Skills
Collaboration, Ensemble Play, Following

Awareness

A great warm-up and focusing game that also explores timing, group energy and ensemble movement.

Start, Stop, Suspension: The Players roam around the room randomly, adjusting so the entire group is moving at the same speed. When this is achieved, the Guide hits a drum: *everyone stops simultaneously, every part of their bodies goes still*. The Guide hits a drum and the group starts moving again simultaneously. They try to match pace, stop and start a few more times following cues from the Guide. Then the Guide cues the stop with the drum, but the group starts on their own simultaneously, without a cue from the Guide. Then they stop simultaneously without a cue and the Guide signals the start. Finally, the group stops and starts on their own without any cues from the Guide. This is when the Players must communicate with their bodies and sense the subtle clues expressed to cue the start or stop. They watch, listen, and respond, so that all react together, moving or stopping at exactly the same moment as a group.

Add a suspension, the group trying to pause their movement all at once, then continuing. A suspension is a slowing down to the point of almost stopping. A suspension can be turned into a game, a tease that can create tension and expectation. Will the group stop? When will they start moving again at a normal speed, run, go into slow motion?

Add everyone breaking into a run, then stopping, then running, simultaneously without cues from the Guide.

One Go: Everyone stands still except one Player, who walks or runs. As soon as that Player stops, someone in the group must walk or run. *Only one Player moves*. If two Players move, they quickly decide who will stop and who will keep moving (they don't discuss it, one Player simply chooses to stand still while the other keeps moving).

One Stop: Everyone walks or runs except one Player who stands still. As soon as that Player walks or runs, someone in the group stops. *Only one Player stops.* If two stop, they quickly decide who will move and who will stand still.

Progression Start: Everyone stands still except for one Player who runs. As soon as that Player stops, two other Players run simultaneously. When those two stop simultaneously, three Players run simultaneously. This pattern continues until all are running (some who stop will start to run again to attain the increase in numbers). Then all stop at the same time, start again and stop, without cues from the Guide. The Guide can call out the number progression if the Players lose track.

Progression Stop: Everyone is moving except for one Player who stands still. As soon as that Player moves, two other Players stop simultaneously. When those two move simultaneously, three other Players stop. This pattern continues until all have stopped (some who move will stop again to attain the increase in numbers). Then all start at the same time, stop, start and stop once more to end the game.

Note: Stops, starts and suspensions, when used in duos, trios or groups, are useful in clowning for creating expectations and tension, setting up and drawing attention to an action, and creating moments of playful synchronicity.

Side-coaching

The Players should be reminded to stay energised when standing still, to use the starts, stops and suspensions to tune in to the group.

+ Drum

Skills
Breath Work, Collaboration, Ensemble Play, Listening, Timing, Warm-Up

8 — ENERGY

Breath and Movement

An effective way to link breath with movement and use it to connect the ensemble.

Breathe, Walk, Breathe: The Players imagine a string tied to the crown of their head pulling their spine tall, the body hanging from this string, relaxed, eyes looking straight ahead. They breathe: on the inhalation, rather than *pulling* the breath into the lungs, the Players imagine their body opening up so the breath can *fall* into the lungs, filling the body; on the exhalation, they let the breath fall out of the lungs. The objective is to breathe deeply to release tension while using as little effort as possible.

At the start of the fourth exhalation, the Players walk (imagining the string supporting them), stopping when they run out of breath. As they inhale, the Players look for a new direction in which to walk (they don't stop looking until the inhalation is complete). On the exhalation, they walk.

Repeat a few times, then the group tries to time their breathing so they all start and stop together. If someone runs out of breath before the others, they stop. Or if they have enough air, they keep going, then try to re-time their breathing to match the group. If a Player doesn't end up in sync, they don't force it; they just keep focusing on their breathing and their movement.

Note: The Players explore ways to use the breath to achieve balance, precision, poise and presence. They want to find a flow between the inhalation/standing still, and the exhalation/moving.

Like stops, starts and suspensions, conscious use of the breath can be used in clowning for drawing attention to an action, and creating eccentric ways of moving.

Breath Matches Movement: The Players match different ways of breathing to different ways of moving: short, held, in-breaths with short stops, a series of short out-breaths with short movements.

In- and out-breaths are matched with staccato stops and starts or jerky movements. They could follow deep inhalations with a series of jumps or long strides. They match the breathing to the movement it suggests, always moving on the exhalation, stopping and looking on the inhalation.

This can be explored individually, or with the entire group using the same method of breathing and moving.

8

ENERGY

Skills
Breath Work, Collaboration, Ensemble Play, Listening, Timing, Warm-Up

9

Count Up, Count Down

A good game for working with energy and movement as a group, and introducing minimum-to-MAXIMUM.

Warm-Up: The Players do a vocal warm-up, working the voice up and down the scale, soft and loud in volume.

The Count: Groups of seven Players lie face-down in a circle, heads pointing towards the centre. One Player starts by striking a pose (rising up slightly, or just lifting a hand) and saying 'One' in a low, barely audible voice (he holds the pose until the count comes around to him again). The Player to his left strikes a different, slightly larger pose and says in a slightly louder voice 'Two.'

This continues around the circle, each Player striking a pose one step up (bigger) than the previous Player, the number spoken in a louder voice, the volume matching the pose. They keep going until someone tops out, creating a pose so big and a count so loud that the next Player can't top it. He then starts back down the scale, until the last Player's pose is low to the ground, his voice barely audible.

The Players lie face-down and begin a new round with a different Player starting.

Note: The count will usually go around the circle a few times before it peaks, so each Player will get more than one turn.

Speed Count: Same as above, but the Players do it quickly, each pose like a flash photograph being taken, the count, soft to LOUD! and back down again.

Side-coaching

- The build from minimum-to-MAXIMUM is gradual so the Players shouldn't go too big too soon.

- How clear can the Players make the changes so the increase and decrease builds as a series of sharp movements and sounds?

- How subtle can the Players make changes so the increase and decrease *flows* from one movement and sound to the next?

9

ENERGY

Skills
Collaboration, Ensemble Play, Following, Listening, minimum-to-MAXIMUM, Warm-Up

10 Ha-Ha-Ha! Wah-Wah-Wah…

ENERGY

This game explores the infectious nature of laughing and crying, and how they're connected to our breathing. It's also a great way to release tension and get the whole group laughing!

Warm-Up: The Players stand in a circle facing in. They shake out their bodies, especially the shoulders. They coordinate their breathing, inhaling and exhaling audibly together, four times. Then they say 'Ha-ha-ha-ha…' on the exhalation until they're out of breath. They repeat this a few times, then exhale with 'Wah-wah-wah-wah…' It's fine if laughter breaks out or the Players exaggerate the weeping quality of 'Wah-wah-wah-wah…' The warm-up is meant to get the breath flowing, working the lungs and the torso.

Progression: Five Players wait backstage. The Guide shows a hand signal to cue them when to exit during the scene to be played, then sets five chairs next to each other, facing the audience. The Players enter and sit. They have a glint in their eyes like they've just heard the funniest joke ever, but the rest of their faces and bodies give nothing away (no big smiles).

The Player sitting on the stage-left end turns to his right with a happy glint in his eye, makes eye contact with the next Player, who responds with a slight grin. He shows this to the audience then makes eye contact with the next Player. She smiles broadly, shares her smile with the audience and turns to her right. The next Player starts chuckling softly. He shares this with the audience then turns right. The fifth Player laughs audibly. He shares this with the audience and turns left, passing the energy back down the line.

As it works its way up and down the line, each Player raises the level until the entire group is convulsed with laughter! The Guide lets them explore this energy to see what comes out of the varied, boisterous laughter, then signals the exit.

The group continues laughing as they leave and keeps laughing backstage until the Guide comes and signals them to end it.

Note: Having the Players exit still laughing keeps the energy flowing all the way offstage; it becomes less of a formal, group exercise. I have found that some Players don't really let loose with their laughter until they're out of sight of the audience. I've pulled back the curtain on some groups revealing them still laughing which causes everyone to laugh more!

Laughter to Tears: Same as *Progression* above, but when it returns to the starting Player, he takes it down a notch and passes it back. When it returns to the starting Player again, he changes that happy glint in his eye to a sad look on his face. This energy progresses down the line until the whole group is weeping loudly 'Wah-wah-wah-wah!' When it gets back to the starting Player, he takes the weeping down a notch and passes it back, the group progresses from weeping to that happy glint in their eyes, until they're back to a full-on belly laugh.

They play these progressions of laughing and crying up and down the line. The Guide cues the exit with the Players still laughing or weeping. They continue backstage until the Guide comes and signals them to end it.

Note: The Players don't have to sit for the entire exercise. They can move about, switch chairs, go with what they feel in the moment to help with the breathing, the release and the play with the ensemble.

Side-coaching

- If laughing or crying don't come easily, the Players should force it; better an exaggerated fake laugh or weeping than resistance; the fake laughter/crying can be used to break through to find a flow.
- The Players can say the words 'Ha-ha-ha!' or 'Wah-wah-wah…' This fake laugh/cry might even cause others to laugh/cry at a Player's efforts!

ENERGY

10

- It's hard to openly laugh or weep if the breath isn't flowing, and if there is tension in the torso. Encourage the Players to shake their arms, stretch their faces, move their bodies while doing the exercise. These actions may also generate laughter.

+ Bench, couch or chairs for 5 players
Skills
Breath Work, Collaboration, Ensemble Play, Following, minimum-to-MAXIMUM

PART TWO

PLAY

Creating connections through physical play

Most people, when they hear the word 'play', think of something frivolous, distracting, entertaining – not serious nor practical. Yet real play requires thoughtful action – the Players must know and follow the rules, stay safe in the midst of vigorous activity, pay attention to other bodies, objects and the space they're playing in. They also have to be ready, willing and able to bend or even break the rules, up-end what is going on to enhance the experience for themselves and others.

Play is a complex activity, both fun and serious, rigorous and ridiculous, an opportunity to succeed through skill, willpower or luck, but also fail honestly, deliberately, exuberantly, in order to expand the possibilities of a game or scene.

It is through lively and sometimes ferocious play that we raise the level of energy and connect with one another on a more dynamic level.

To think like a clown is to see the potential for play in every idea, movement, prop, costume, scene, and in every partner. The Players get to a point at which play is not an activity indulged in now-and-then, but is the visible outcome of their constant state of mind. This is clowning.

We can study clowns throughout history and in various cultures, examine different comic archetypes, read about the lives of various practitioners, but to truly understand the potential of clowning and why it has held such a fascination for so many cultures, we have to get on our feet and play.

Let's Dance

A full-body warm-up that gets the Players moving in a myriad of ways to various styles of music. These variations combine skill, spatial awareness, physical improvisation and ensemble play.

Note: It's a good idea to avoid music with vocals (unless it's in a language that the Players don't understand), or songs that are popular; the Players should respond to the music not to the lyrics or their associations with a hit tune.

If you have gym mats, spread them out so the Players can roll, stretch, dance on hands and knees, etc. Below are some suggested dance themes.

Warm-Up: The Players dance on their own to stretch and warm up the body. This is a good way to start any session.

Isolations: The Guide calls out parts of the body. The Players isolate and dance with just that part, shifting from one to the other as the Guide calls out another part. The Guide hits a drum and the Players progress from dancing with one part, letting that spread to other parts, until their whole body is dancing.

Back-to-Back: The Players partner up and maintain contact back-to-back as they dance. They change partners by making eye contact with another pair, press shoulders against shoulders, then quarter turn and roll onto the back of a new partner, switching partners as they make contact with a new back.

Soul Train Line: The group forms two lines facing each other, three metres apart. The Players spread out so each line is at least six metres long. A Player from each line, opposite each other, steps into the centre between the lines at their end, and the two of them dance, showing off their moves as they strut their way down between the lines. The others encourage them, feed them positive energy. When the duo reaches the opposite end from where they started, they point back to the start, cueing two more Players into the centre (the Players who've just danced step back in at the end of the line). This is based on the *Soul Train* line from the iconic music and dance show.

Cool/Loony Dance: The Players dance as smooth and cool as they can be, then lose their cool and get loony, then struggle to get back to being cool and on beat. They keep switching, making the contrast strong between ultra-cool to completely ridiculous!

Body-Part Touching: The Players partner up and dance, always maintaining contact with a part of the body: hand-to-hand, forehead-to-back, foot held in partner's hand, a wrist held in the crook of partner's elbow, etc. They can switch partners by making eye contact with another duo, establishing a new point of physical contact, then dancing off with their new partner. Try in groups of three, five, or the whole group dancing together, always maintaining a point of physical contact.

Prop/Clothes Partner: The Players dance with an article of clothing; it can be animated, danced with like a puppet partner, or used in a flashy, expressive way to accent the dancing.

Evocative: The Guide plays slow, evocative music and the Players move to it.

Tense/Loose Dance: The Players dance with their whole body tensed up. The Guide hits a drum once to signal the Players to switch to dancing with the body rag-doll loose. With each hit of the drum they switch, tense to loose, and back again.

Big Cheese: The Guide gives a ball or hat to a Player, making them the *Big Cheese*, the supreme leader of the dance. The others follow the Big Cheese, in awe of everything she does, nearly overwhelmed to be dancing with her! At some point, the Big Cheese passes the ball or hat to another Player. The transition is important: it's a big deal to be designated the new Big Cheese! The group worships the new Big Cheese as they all dance around him. Each one passes on the title, until everyone has had a chance to be the Big Cheese and lead the dance.

Obstacle-Course Disco: If mats, furniture and large soft objects (see below for ideas) are available, set these around the room to create obstacles, levels and provide toys that the Players can jump on, roll over, scramble under, toss around to each other, etc., while they dance.

+ Music player and a playlist, gym mats, soft props (exercise balls, blankets, foam pool noodles, durable hats and coats), and a drum (use a drumstick or hit it with the hand)

Skills
Ensemble Play, Following, Leading, Physical Expression, Warm-Up

Alien, Cow, Lion

A good game for connecting the ensemble and encouraging playfulness.

The Players stand in a circle, each one silently choosing a role:

- *Alien* holds index fingers next to their head like short antennae, curls their index fingers up and down, and says 'Bloop-bloop.'
- *Cow* holds right wrist against their tummy, fingers extended (the udders), wriggles their fingers and says 'Moooo.'
- *Lion* shakes their head as if rustling their hairy mane while saying 'Roar!'

The Guide claps; every Player snaps into their chosen role. The objective is for everyone to become the same role on the clap (with no one hinting what they will choose beforehand).

Play a few times; then play so the majority wins and roles that are in the minority have to step out. The game continues until all the Players that are left snap in to the same animal on the clap.

Skills
Collaboration, Ensemble Play, Introductions, Listening, Warm-Up

Mouse, Cat, Dog, Horse, Eagle

A good physical warm-up for building energy and encouraging group play.

Test Run: The Players form a circle. The Guide starts; he lifts his left foot, then his right, as if a mouse is running under his feet. As soon as he puts down his right foot, the Player to his right lifts her left foot, then her right as if the mouse is running under her feet. This continues around the circle.

When it gets back to the Guide, he lifts his left foot, then his right higher (knees up towards chest), as if a big cat is running under his feet. The Player to his right does the same as the big cat runs under her feet. This continues around the circle.

When it gets back to the Guide, he jumps up (both feet at the same time), as if a dog is running under his feet. When he lands, the Player to his right jumps. This continues around the circle.

When it gets back to the Guide, he looks left and leans back with his upper body then steps back with his left foot then his right, as if a horse is running past, then steps forward, left foot, right, and finishes by looking to his right. This triggers the next Player's movement. This continues around the circle.

When it gets back to the Guide, he looks left, raises his arms shoulder high and ducks into a squat, as if an eagle is flying overhead, chasing the other animals. He rises back up and looks right, triggering the next Player. This continues around the circle.

Fast Chase: The game starts the same as above, but when the mouse reaches the third Player from the Guide, the Guide lifts his feet for the cat. When the cat reaches the third Player from the Guide, the Guide jumps for the dog, etc. In this variation, the Players are constantly reacting to the animals chasing each other rather than waiting for each one to go all the way around the circle.

Mouse! Cat! Dog! Horse! Eagle!: Same as *Fast Chase* above, but as the animals pass, each Player shouts the name of the animal going by. Start slow and speed up, trying to keep track of the animals and the physical reaction, while remembering to call out its name.

Note: The Guide should emphasise accuracy in the movements at the start and give the Players a few moments to practise the movements for each animal. If it gets a little muddled as it speeds up, that's part of the play.

Skills
Clarity, Ensemble Play, Introductions, Timing, Warm-Up

Clap It Round

This game explores rhythm, group play, and connecting with partners using sound and breath.

Clap, Raspberry, Oh!: The Players stand in a circle. The Guide turns to the Player to his left and says 'One.' That Player then turns to his left and says 'Two.' The next Player turns left and says 'Three.' The next player starts the three-count over again. Run this pattern around the circle a few times, increasing the speed with each round.

The Guide starts again. This time any Player saying 'One' claps instead of saying the number. Try this a few times. Then any Player saying 'Two' substitutes a raspberry (sticking their tongue out, making a fart sound); so the Guide claps, the next Player does the raspberry, the next Player says 'Three.' Try this a few times around the circle, then any Player saying 'Three' says 'Oh!' instead; so the Guide claps, the next Player does the raspberry, the next Player says 'Oh!', the next Player claps, etc. Try this around the circle playing with speed and timing.

Note: Any percussive movement such as stomping the foot or a vocal noise such as 'Mmmm...' or 'Ah!' can be substituted for the numbers once the group runs the one-two-three.

Clap Together: The Players stand in a circle. The starting Player turns to her left, makes eye contact with the next Player, and they clap in unison. The next Player then turns to the Player to his left, makes eye contact, and they clap in unison. Continue clockwise around the circle. Try various speeds: pass it fast or in slow motion, open hands wide before clapping, or just enough to make a sound.

Once the Players have run the clap around the circle a few times, they can reverse it: instead of turning and passing the clap clockwise, the Player stays facing the one who passed the clap and claps back at her (they clap in unison). The one who gets it back now turns right and passes the clap anticlockwise. Or they can clap back at the Player who just passed it back, forcing her to pass it around the circle clockwise. The Player can also turn to pass to her left but then turn back and clap at the Player who passed it.

Encourage Players to get creative: drop to their knees and clap, jump up and clap, do a pirouette and clap, etc. This requires the Player to telegraph or wind up to the move so she and her partner can do it in unison. Avoid words! The Players should use their eyes and actions to cue their partner and keep trying until they clap together.

Clap, Pass, Breathe: The Players stand in a circle. The starting Player is the *Clapper*. He 'throws a clap' to the Player to his right as he exhales, clapping his hands together in front of his mouth and extending both hands towards the Player in sync with his breath. The *Receiver* (ready with arms extended), then claps her hands and brings them towards her face as she inhales, receiving the clap. Receiver then becomes Clapper and sends a clap to the person to her right. The Players coordinate the breath and the movement, exhaling with the clap and throwing it, inhaling with the clap and receiving it. This continues around the circle.

Play with different speeds, always keeping the clap in sync with the breath and the movement.

They can also reverse it as above by clapping right back at the person who passed it (Clapper should stay ready with arms extended in case it gets passed back to them).

Skills
Breath Work, Collaboration, Introductions, Timing, Warm-Up

Chase and Tag

These variations on the game of Tag are good warm-ups and they immediately immerse the Players in active, physical play.

Preparation: In the first variations the Players will need a clear path to the walls at opposite ends of the room. Clear the playing area of any objects the Players might stumble over.

Heads and Tails, Hear It: The Players divide into two equal teams. The Guide marks a line with rope in the centre of the room. Each team stands a metre from the line facing each other. The wall behind each team is the *Safe Zone*: to be safe, the Players must be touching the wall. One team is designated *Heads*, the other, *Tails*. The Guide flips a coin and calls it. Whichever team is called chases the other, trying to tag the Players before they get to the Safe Zone. If a Player is tagged she freezes in place. Once Players have been tagged or reached their wall, those who were tagged join the other team on their side and the game starts again. This continues until all the Players end up on one team (if time allows).

Heads and Tails, See It: Same as above, but teams are given a number, *One* and *Two*. The Guide marks a flat plastic or metal plate with 1 on one side, 2 on the other. The Guide flips the plate off to one side so it's not in the way but still visible by some of the Players. Rather than hearing the call, the Players see it; whichever number is showing, that team chases the other (i.e. if 2 is visible, Team Two chases Team One). Some Players will see it sooner than others. Those who are further away from the plate should look to their teammates to know how to respond: if they see their partners run for the wall, they know they're being chased. This continues until all the Players end up on one team.

Hold-the-Chicken Tag: Pass out three rubber chickens (or knotted towels) for eight or more Players. One Player is *Tagger*; she can tag any Player except those holding chickens – holding a chicken keeps you safe. If a Player sees someone about to be tagged, she can throw or hand off a chicken to them. If a Player is tagged he joins Taggers. This continues until all but one are tagged (eliminate the chickens as the number of Taggers increases until there is only one left for two people). The only Player left holding a chicken becomes the new Tagger, starting a new game. Chickens are off-limits to Taggers. They cannot intercept them.

Hold-the-Chicken Tag Timed: To keep the Players from holding the chicken too long, the Guide can set a time limit and have the Players count. As soon as they get a chicken they count out loud, 'Four – Three – Two – One.' On 'one' they must get rid of the chicken. This produces a more energetic game and leads to some creative passing.

Add: If a chicken is thrown and a Tagger intercepts it, she removes it from the game, leaving one less chicken to keep the Players safe.

Band-Aid Tag: One Player is *Tagger*. Whenever he tags someone, they hold a hand (the Band-Aid) over the place where they were tagged. When someone gets tagged three times, they've run out of Band-Aids (hands) and have to freeze until one or more Players operate on them. They place a hand over each of the frozen Player's Band-Aids and say, 'Heal!' allowing the frozen Player to rejoin the game. The Tagger should tag the Players in difficult-to-reach places, ones that make it more challenging to run around while keeping a hand on the spot, e.g. the back of the knee. The Tagger can't make three tags in a row on a single player. They tag the Player then move to another, then back.

+ A coin to flip; a plate with number 1 written on one side, 2 written on the other, three rubber chickens or thick knotted towels; two metres of rope

Skills
Competition, Ensemble Play, Warm-Up

Eyes Closed

Games played with eyes closed are important for developing the Players' other senses. They become more focused and learn to listen not only with their ears but also with their bodies.

Preparation: As the Players will work with their eyes closed, ensure there is nothing to trip over, or hard or sharp objects they could walk into or step on.

Doo-Wee: The Players close their eyes and roam. When they bump into another Player they shake hands with each other, and both ask 'Doo-Wee?' This tells them that neither is Doo-Wee, so they keep on roaming.

The Guide squeezes the shoulder of one Player designating them *Doo-Wee*. She continues to roam (eyes still closed), but when a Player bumps into her, grabs her hand to shake it and asks 'Doo-Wee?' she remains silent. The silence tells the Player he has found Doo-Wee. He holds one hand of Doo-Wee and they walk side-by-side. The next Player who bumps into them finds a free hand to shake and asks, 'Doo-Wee?' They remain silent so she joins hands with them, moving down the line of held hands with eyes closed until she finds a free hand. This continues until all become Doo-Wee, all holding hands, walking side by side.

Note: The Guide should remind the Players to listen well in order to locate the silent Doo-Wee.

Werewolf: All players start as *Victims*. They keep their eyes closed as they roam. Guide squeezes the shoulder of a Victim to designate her *Werewolf*. When she bumps into someone, she grabs Victim's shoulders and howls. Victim screams 'Noooooo!' then he becomes a Werewolf too. If two Werewolves grab one another, they both howl, then move on. Continue until all are Werewolves.

Werewolf Freeze: When a Werewolf grabs a Victim and howls, the Victim screams 'Noooooo!'

and freezes in place. If a Werewolf grabs someone she has already frozen, Victim stays silent and Werewolf moves on. This continues until all are frozen. Eyes remain closed throughout the game.

Add: If a Victim finds a frozen Victim, he takes their hand and says 'Live.' This unfreezes them and they rejoin the game.

Side-coaching

Encourage the Players to explore the power that comes with being a Werewolf, as well as the helplessness that comes with being a Victim; the fear of being caught by a Werewolf is mixed with the curiosity about becoming one and gaining power over others.

Skills
Ensemble Play, Listening, Trust, Warm-Up

You–Me

A game of give-and-take that encourages the Players to react physically to one another, combining movement with words.

You–Me: The Players stand in a circle. The Guide turns in a clockwise direction and says 'You' to the Player to her left. The Player to her left then turns to his own left and says 'You' to the next Player.

This continues around the circle. The Players explore pace – normal, fast or slow – and play with their movements as they turn and say 'You.'

Now add 'Me.' After a Player turns and says 'You', the Player to his left says 'Me' then turns to his left and says 'You.' The next Player replies 'Me.' This continues around the circle.

The Players explore different ways of saying the words – as a question, an accusation, saying it seductively, sweetly, happily, suspiciously, etc.

They *throw* the word 'You' with the body – point with the fingers, gesture with the hands, thrust the head or pelvis forward, push out the chest, point with a foot, etc.

As the Players respond with 'Me', they physicalise *catching* the word. For example, the chest contracts, the hands protect their face, they turn their torso away as they say 'Me.'

'You' has a forward, expanding energy; 'Me' has a retreating, contracting one.

You–Me Reverse: For this variation, after a Player turns in a clockwise direction and says 'You' to the Player to his left, she can reverse directions by answering 'You' right back. He responds with 'Me' and sends the game around the circle anticlockwise.

Or he can answer with another 'You' giving it back to her. Or they exchange a series of 'You' until one of them says 'Me' and starts the game moving around the circle.

The Players keep the physicality in the throwing of 'You' and the catching of 'Me.'

Note: This kind of physicalisation can be used for any routine or scene and with any verbal exchange. This sort of give-and-take is an important part of clowning as it's primarily a visual and physical art form.

Skills
Ensemble Play, Following, Listening, Warm-Up

Game On

The play that is generated by this game is infectious. It's one of the best games I know of for uniting a group and revealing the potential of improvised ensemble play.

To start, the Guide says 'Begin'; to stop, she crosses her arms and says 'The end.' Make this clear at the start or students might never stop playing!

The Players form a circle and relax their bodies and faces, arms at their sides. The Guide says 'Begin.'

The game can be as simple as a Player scratching their nose, inhaling audibly, moving their left hand or smiling. The other Players see this first game, everyone copies it, until all are playing this game.

The Players now have two choices: if all are smiling (for example), they can evolve the game – smiling might lead to laughing which could lead to the Players pointing at each other and laughing harder; or they can start another game – a Player introduces something new, such as jumping up and down – and the group flows into playing it.

The Players can vocalise as well as break away from the circle and move about the room, but they must stay focused on the group to pick up any new game that is introduced.

If two Players introduce a game at the same time, the group decides which game to play. The majority rules: any Player who introduces a game that isn't chosen must join the group rather than cling to or force their idea on the ensemble.

To end, the Guide plays the game of bringing the Players into a circle, crosses her arms and says 'The end.'

Note: The listening that is required by this game is crucial to clowning, especially in regard to improvisation and ensemble devising. The Players learn not only to tune in to each other but gain confidence that if they truly listen, ideas will come to them.

Side-coaching

The Players let the action develop organically as they focus on *not* leading – no one needs to force anything. It's a game of waiting and listening in order to connect with the ensemble.

Skills
Collaboration, Ensemble Play, Following, Improvisation, Listening, Trust, Warm-Up

Buf Da

One of the best games I know for exploring group rhythm, timing, learning to stay calm in the midst of group activity, and being able to take the lead in a game or scene.

One Leader, One Ball: The Players stand in a circle, arm's length apart. *Leader* stands in the middle holding a ball. Leader and the Players toss the ball back and forth saying 'Buf' on the throw and 'Da' on the catch (the ball always goes from Leader to a Player in the circle and back again – never from Player to Player). All the Players (including Leader) time the words so they say 'Buf' at *exactly* the same moment as they throw, and 'Da' at *exactly* the same moment as they catch. This timing is crucial in later variations. Everyone works to create a rhythmic connection between sound, throw and catch.

Any Player can take over from Leader by stepping into the circle and placing a hand on Leader's shoulder (make it a prolonged contact, not a tap). This is the signal they want to lead. The old Leader joins the circle, the new Leader takes over without stopping the game: the Players in the circle time their throws so that the new Leader can take over seamlessly.

Once the Players get the hang of it, let Leader get three to five throws, then a new Leader takes over. This keeps the exchange between Leader and the Players active and lively. Make sure everyone takes a turn at being Leader.

One Leader, Two Balls: Played as above but the Players toss two balls. Start with one ball in the hands of Leader, one in the hands of a Player in the circle. Throws are timed so that as one ball goes out to a Player, another comes back to Leader: neither Leader nor Player should ever end up with two balls. Any Player can become the new Leader as above. Say 'Buf' and 'Da' loud and clear, so that Leader knows where the balls are coming from, and all the Players know where they're going to.

Buf Da Chaos: One Leader in the centre, two balls. The Players don't maintain a circle but move around Leader in a random way, weaving around each other, some running, some standing still. Balls always go from Leader to the Players, never from Player to Player. This is when all elements are crucial: the words 'Buf' and 'Da' spoken loudly, timed *exactly* on the throw and catch, said with the intention of getting Leader's attention. The Players must stay focused on where the balls are at all times. Any Player can become the new Leader, as above.

Side-coaching

- Leaders can control the rhythm and speed of the game. If they feel bewildered, they can slow it down and prompt the group to play at a more relaxed pace. If they feel playful, they can speed up the exchange, challenge the group with how they throw, roll, bounce or hand off the ball. This is a chance to learn to *own* the role of Leader.

- The Players in the circle must support each Leader's way of playing. Some will be focused and skilled, others overwhelmed and awkward. The Players must adjust the rhythm and pace of their game according to each Leader's ability. At the same time, they should challenge Leader with how they throw, roll, bounce or hand off the ball, always sensitive to Leader's response. It's a *collaborative* game not a competition.

- This game is effective in understanding timing, tempo and rhythm, and how to be a leader and control the play or scene by establishing pace and focus; it also shows the Players how to play with and provoke – and support – a leader, while staying aware of others in a scene.

+ Two balls (volleyballs, Nerf or playground balls work best). Don't use anything too light, small or hard

Skills
Clarity, Collaboration, Ensemble Play, Following, Leading, Listening, Timing, Warm-Up

PART THREE

CURIOSITY

Encouraging listening as well as imaginative, improvised play

When talking about clowning, many practitioners will use words like 'vulnerable', 'innocent', 'stupid' and 'honest'. I'd like to add '*curious*'. Curiosity is a *forward* energy: clowns enter the performance space looking to the audience to see who wants to engage with them, relate to them, play with them!

This curiosity isn't limited to the animate; clowns see potential partners in the clothes they wear, a chair, a ball, a stick, a carrot – even the walls and floor.

The characteristics we often associate with clowns – a sense of wonder, openness, awkwardness, slapstick comedy, rambunctious activity, a desire to test limits – are all born from this curiosity. 'Why can't I push that button, the one with the sign that says "DON'T PUSH THIS BUTTON!" What will happen if I do? I *must* know.'

Unlike the jester, agitprop comedian or satirist, clowns are naive about rules and the 'right way' to do things; they don't *deliberately* break a law or up-end an established order, it's just that their curiosity and their desire to engage with the world are more powerful than any rule or boundary! The clown is less an agitated rebel, more of an overeager explorer.

These exercises focus on listening and observing, provoking curiosity in order to lead the Players towards imaginative, improvised play.

20 Wide-Eyed

CURIOSITY

This is a good exercise for encouraging the Players to see the world with fresh eyes, letting go of their preconceptions and expectations.

The Players scatter about the room and lie on their backs with their eyes closed. They take four deep breaths as they listen to the sounds around them. After the fourth exhalation, the Guide tells them to open their eyes and explore the space and everything in it *as if for the first time*.

They avoid interacting with each other: their curiosity is focused on the room – the walls, the floor, the ceiling – and the objects in it. They shouldn't get too involved in any one thing: their curiosity leads them around the entire room, making them eager to explore everything in it. How do things look, smell, feel, sound?

To end, the Guide says 'Rest.' The Players lie down and close their eyes, breathing deeply four times. The group gathers in a circle and the Guide asks:

> Were you able to find an openness to the room so you could experience things for the first time? Or did you find yourself *playing* at being open and curious?
>
> Were you able to achieve a feeling of seeing everything for the first time, not knowing what things were or what they were used for? How did that feel?
>
> Were you able to engage with things in a fresh, unknowing way, making discoveries about what they could be, rather than what you know them to be?

Note: This kind of openness is important for clowning, as it enables a Player to enter into any routine or scene and recreate it afresh every time. It can also help them invent new uses for everyday objects and transform the pedestrian into something imaginative.

Side-coaching

- The things in the room do not evoke a strong emotional response, they simply make the Players curious. They explore a bit and move on. They don't get indulgent with any one thing.

- The objective is not to play dumb or act like a kid, but to get back to a 'beginner's mind', exploring the space and the objects, seeing them for the first time, not knowing what they are or how they're used. The Players don't know the purpose of a chair, what to do with a ball, a door, etc. They explore them at a sensory level, their shape, texture, the sounds they make, their smell, etc.

- This exercise about training the mind to see the world without preconceptions or expectations, exploring without imposing anything on the space or the things in it.

Skills
Clarity, Improvisation, Listening, Warm-Up

Point of Focus

21

This exercise has elements of neutral mask work. It's a good way to practise giving attention to something so that the audience sees it clearly.

Focus, Move, Stop: The Players stand anywhere in the room. They breathe deeply, relaxing their bodies. They're alert but without tension. They search for a point to focus on. When they see it, they use a series of movements to make their point of focus obvious to an observer; for example, if the Player sees something to her right, her head turns, following the eyes, the body follows the head. It's a series of three separate movements from small (eyes only) to large (head), to largest (whole body). The movement of the body can also be separated into chest turning, solar plexus turning, and finally pelvis turning legs to face the point of focus. The Player should make sure her feet turn as well.

Keeping their eyes fixed on the point, *after* they fully turn, the Player walks to it. When she arrives, she comes to a complete stop. After stopping, she finds another point of focus, and with the eyes leading the head, the head leading the body, she turns, *then* moves towards this new point. The Player repeats this, moving to a series of focus points, staying fully aware of her movements as a series of isolations.

Energy Pull: Once the Players have a good understanding of *Focus, Move, Stop*, they add an *internal* shift: the point of focus invokes curiosity. The Players feel *pulled* towards the focal point once they lock their gaze on it. It's subtle, a *feeling* of being drawn to the point of focus rather than only showing it with an obvious physical movement. The Players centre this pull in the solar plexus, midway between the navel and the base of the sternum. This is where the walk towards the object starts from, this strong desire to interact with the thing that the eyes see.

Note: The first variation is more of a movement exercise, whereas the second works more with the emotions, with curiosity and desire.

This physical clarity can be incorporated into any routine or scene to draw focus to an object or a partner, or to misdirect the audience's attention to set up a moment somewhere else onstage.

Side-coaching

- The point of focus can be on the wall, the floor, or an object in the room. The Players don't fix their gaze on another person.

- The Players don't exaggerate their reactions or create a scene. They explore body isolations and movement towards the point of focus without embellishing.

- The stop is an energised state: the body is alert, its attention fixed on a point outside of itself. Curiosity about what it sees gives the body a presence, an aliveness that is not based on exaggeration but an internal feeling of openness, ready to respond to each discovery.

Skills
Breath Work, Clarity, Physical Expression, Warm-Up

22 Takes

CURIOSITY

In physical theatre, a 'take' is more than just a look, it's a way of playing with how you see something and how you react. The take and the reaction can reveal something about a Player, the thing they're looking at, and their relationship to it. Takes can develop and expand any moment in a scene.

Warm-Up: The Players spread out. The Guide sets props around the room at different levels. The Players move around the room practising takes, exploring variations in seeing an object and reacting to what they see. They can see it, react and move on, or move towards the object (they don't touch or handle it), pause, take to another object, and move on. The Guide reads from the list below, leading the Players through various takes:

The eyes see it, the head moves and turns the entire body until you face the object. Walk to it.

The eyes see it, the head moves, but the rest of the body pulls you in another direction. Play with this tension: the eye's strong desire to look, the body's strong desire to move on.

Do a double-take, a triple-take. Vary the timing between each take; for example, see it, look away for a few seconds, perhaps take a step, then look again. Vary the reactions as well; react after the first take with surprise, after the second with anger.

You want to take, but you only pause, never fully turning to look. Tease the audience with *almost* looking.

Play with size. Make the take and the reaction subtle, a small change in posture or a slight intake of the breath. Or the whole body reacts and the take leads to a jump in the air, a cartwheel, a short dance, etc.

When you see the object, the entire body contracts, drawing in on itself, exhaling completely. Now do a take and expand, puffing yourself up, widening your stance, inhaling deeply.

When you see the object, the reaction is vocal as well as physical (a sound, not a word). The sound can be short or continued until you look away or exit. Use the sound to express how you feel about seeing the object.

After you see the object, step forward and do something – point or wave at it, stick out your tongue, etc.

The back 'sees' the object, stops the body, and pulls the head around. Try it with other parts of the body – the left shoulder, the pelvis, both hands, etc. Let that part of the body move first. For example, push the pelvis towards the object. This movement turns the rest of the body. Or the feet both turn to look, so you look down at the feet to see what the feet are looking at, then look at the object.

Play with the spine: seeing the object lengthens the spine, you grow taller. Or it compresses the spine, shrinks you. It twists the spine, bends it back or forward. Or the reaction travels from your eyes down your spine in an undulation.

React from a specific place. For example, the eyes see it and the pelvis wiggles (keep the rest of the body still); or the eyes see it and the fingers flutter.

Play with timing and pace: the take happens right after entering; or it happens after you walk past the object. Try a quick entrance leading to a slow take and vice versa.

Solo Takes: Three Players wait backstage. The Guide sets up two stage flats (or curtains) to create places for entrances and exits, with a six-metre gap between them. She places an object on the floor or on a small table anywhere downstage of the flats. Three Players wait behind the flats. The first Player enters, does a take to the object, reacts, then exits (they can walk across the stage from one flat to the other, or go back the way they came). The second Player enters as soon as the first exits, does a take to the object, reacts, then exits. When he exits, the third Player enters and goes through the sequence.

They each make three or more passes, doing a take and a reaction on each pass (the Guide decides how many passes they make). Encourage them to use any of the variations from the *Warm-Up* (the Guide can call them out if needed).

Note: This is such a classic physical-comedy skill that some comedians became famous for how they looked at something – Edgar Kennedy's 'slow burn' or Oliver Hardy's forlorn, exasperated takes to the camera (borrowed years later by Jack Benny and Johnny Carson).

Side-coaching

- As soon as a Player exits, the next one comes on immediately. Part of the play is the transition between the Players – how they leave the scene after seeing the object and how the next Player enters on top of that energy. A series of solo moments starts to feel like a trio's act.

- The audience sees the object onstage first, so when a Player takes to it, she and the audience now have something in common: they all see the object. Once the take happens, the crowd becomes curious about how the Player will respond. This anticipation is part of the play between the audience and the Player. How can the Players use this anticipation and tension to connect with the crowd?

+ Stage flats or curtains, various props

Skills
Clarity, Devising, Improvisation, Physical Expression, Solos, Timing, Trios

Chain Reaction

This game can get confusing, intense and quite funny. No one is sure who's leading a movement or the play. Everyone is trying hard to concentrate until even that effort becomes part of the game!

The Players stand in a circle and count off. The Guide sets a pattern for the group, for example, every fourth person. Say there are ten in the group: the first Player watches the fifth, the second Player watches the sixth, the third Player watches the seventh, the fourth Player watches the eighth, the fifth Player watches the ninth, the sixth Player watches the tenth, the seventh Player watches the first, the eighth Player watches the second, the ninth Player watches the third and the tenth Player watches the fourth.

The Guide tells the Players to watch their partner; if they move – even a twitch, a slight move of the head, a shift in how they stand – the one observing should mirror their movement. This sets off a chain reaction as everyone is observing someone else. This can be quite subtle: no one is trying to start anything, the Players are simply responding to visible changes. The instruction 'Don't do anything' allows the Players to focus on each other, respond to movement and energy, and give themselves over to following not leading.

Skills
Ensemble Play, Following, Listening, Warm-Up

24 Entrances and Exits

CURIOSITY

In clown and physical comedy, entire scenes can be created out of nothing more than entrances and exits, so it's crucial that the Players understand how to use them to introduce themselves upon entering, and leave the audience satisfied or curious about who they are when they exit.

Entrances and exits can be used at any time to liven up a scene: there's always the 'threat' that someone may leave, or suddenly enter and change the dynamic. Evocative and hilarious aspects of a relationship – between the Players and with their audience – can be revealed simply by how a Player enters and exits.

The Players should never waste these moments; the Guide should emphasise their importance to the point where strong, playful and imaginative entrances and exits become second nature, and part of every exercise!

Three Players wait backstage. They explore inventive ways to enter. They have a moment onstage (acknowledging the audience with a wave of the hand, a bow, a look, or they can choose not to acknowledge them at all), then find an inventive way to exit. As soon as they exit, the next Player enters, has a moment onstage, then exits. As soon as they exit, the next Player enters, etc. They play the game of entering and exiting until the Guide signals them to stop.

If they don't realise it on their own, the Guide should draw the Players' attention to the curtains or flats; can they enter under them, over them, get stuck in the curtains, knock a flat down or carry it to another part of the stage and then reveal themselves? Find variations in movement, how they use the floor, the walls, how much of their body they reveal in the entrance, etc. They should borrow ideas from each other and develop them further.

Side-coaching

The Guide can side-coach: 'Don't just walk on, cartwheel onstage! Leap on backwards, crawl off. Stagger on weakly, then run off bounding with energy! Come in with a strong emotion. Exit as if there is something offstage you must do. Enter as if someone has thrown you onstage or is chasing you! Exit as if some force is dragging you off. Make us curious about the backstage world you're coming from and where you're going to when you exit.'

Note: Beware of the Player who 'winds up' to performance level after she's entered. Or one whose energy slacks off as he approaches the exit so the last thing the audience sees is him dropping out of the scene.

+ Two stage flats or curtains
Skills
Clarity, Devising, Improvisation, Physical Expression, Solos, Trios

25 The Audience: Hands

This exercise helps develop the Players' ability to listen and respond to the audience in a more direct way.

Three or more Players wait backstage. The Guide can set chairs, a table, a couch, etc., onstage or leave it bare. Two people in the audience are designated as *Me*. The Players make a series of entrances and exits (more than one Player can be onstage). The Players' focus is onstage: they explore the space, the floor, the ceiling, they greet each other, they hang out, improvise a scene, etc., all while continuing to play the game of entering and exiting. They never look out to the audience until a Me raises their hand (both Me can do this at the same time or separately). When a Me gives the signal, all the Players onstage must do a take, looking to that Me.

The Players play with different ways of looking (as explored in *Takes* (Game 22), for as long as a Me has their hand up: the Players do a take, look away, take again, or take to Me, then to each other, then back to Me. If hands are raised by both Me, the Players can take to either one and to each other, or take back and forth between both Me. Takes continue until each Me lowers their hand.

Before the hands go up – and after they go down – all the focus of the Players is on the world onstage. There is a fourth wall and they must not look out. Once a hand goes up, the fourth wall is broken and the Players' attention is always outward, curious, excited, confused, angry, etc., about the world beyond the fourth wall. The hands go down and they're back in the onstage world playing the game of *Entrances and Exits* (Game 24).

Me should play with the timing of the signal. Keep the hand down for longer to tease the Players, making them anxious about when the hand will draw their focus out; or raise and lower it with only a short time in between, generating multiple takes, the Players rapidly switching from the world onstage to the world of the audience.

Side-coaching

- *Timing:* The Players explore when they look out and the quality of the takes: fast, slow, timid, aggressive, etc.
- *Rhythm:* The Players play with how they move their head and body on the take to create rhythmic physical play.
- *Size:* The Players try exaggeration or subtlety. They get big physically, they get small. They explore physical expansion and contraction.
- *Play:* The Players tease the audience with their takes, or let the audience (represented by Me) tease them and make them curious. They make a game of the takes and how they respond once Me raises a hand.
- *Focus:* The Players toy with the intensity of their focus for what's onstage and for what's out in the audience; sometimes they're engrossed by Me to the point of stupidity, other times they're flippant or annoyed.

+ Stage flats or curtains, three or more chairs, a table, a couch

Skills
Clarity, Collaboration, Following, Improvisation, Physical Expression, Timing

26 The Eyes Have It: Choices

This exercise creates obstacles that challenge the Players to find different ways to connect with an audience.

Never Look: Three Players wait backstage. One Player enters, moves to a spot anywhere onstage, pauses, then exits. During this sequence he *never makes eye contact with the audience* from the moment he enters until he exits.

As soon as he exits, another Player enters, also never making eye contact. A third Player enters as soon as the second Player exits, never looking out. They continue, playing the game of *Entrances and Exits* (Game 24), never looking out, until the Guide calls an end to the exercise.

The action of not looking out (not acknowledging the presence of the audience) is referred to as *being*: the Player is in their own world.

Always Look: Same as above, but the Players *always make eye contact with the audience* from the moment they enter until they are completely offstage. The Guide should call out any moments a Player looks away (usually upon entering or to see where the exit is).

The action of always looking out (seeing the audience) is referred to as *being with us*: the Player is in the audience's world.

Choose Your Moment: Same as above, but the Players choose to make eye contact *only once* at any moment in the sequence. It can be as soon as they enter, as they cross the stage, or just before they exit. Only one look is allowed.

The action of choosing their moment to look is referred to as *playing with us*: the Player is knowingly aware of both worlds, the one onstage and the audience's, and plays the game of being in between.

After each group, or after all have gone, the Guide asks:

> As an audience, how do the different ways of using the eyes connect you to the Player?
>
> As the Player, how does your relationship with the audience change with each use of the eyes?
>
> How can you develop the comic and dramatic possibilities of a routine or scene simply by how you use your eyes?

+ Stage flats or curtains

Skills
Devising, Listening, Physical Expression, Solos, Timing

PART FOUR

COMPETITION

Using competition to develop ensemble play

As adults, when we think of play, we usually think *sports*, games that lead to victory or defeat; we associate play with competing. Because of this emphasis on winning – which we're exposed to every hour of every day – one of the things that most people struggle with in a clown class is learning how to fail and to appreciate – even celebrate – failure.

In games of competition, the default energy is usually defensiveness: the Players protect themselves at all costs and become single-minded, all their energy concentrated on success. As a result, the game doesn't expand, doesn't challenge the audience – it remains only Us versus Them. When the Players choose only to defend themselves in order to win, they run the risk of their play becoming predictable: they react rather than relate, block rather than create, guard themselves rather than come forward and play.

A clown, on the other hand, will compete not only against an opponent but against the game itself. They'll actively seek out new tactics (invented on their own or borrowed from others). They might deliberately lose again and again, toy with their opponent's – and the audience's – preconceptions about winning and losing. They might collaborate with those they're competing against, turn their adversary into a partner (while at any moment switch back to competing). Because they aren't focused solely on winning, clowns discover variations on the game and diverse ways to play it: they may be naive or ingenious, sneaky or helpful, pugnacious or subservient, act the hero as well as the martyr, sacrificing themselves to see how that might change the game and our notions of what it means to win and lose. The game then has the potential to become a scene, a story, as the clown invents and plays different games from within the main game.

Competitive games introduce the Players to the importance of tactics, strategies and improvising within a given structure; they also encourage the Players to bend, break and elaborate on those structures, to discover new possibilities.

27

Ha-goo

This game brings out the fun and the crazy in the Players. It's a great exercise for learning how to maintain your focus in the midst of boisterous action.

The Players form two teams, A and B. They face each other with a two-metre gap between them. Each line spreads out so the aisle between the teams is nine metres long. This is the gauntlet.

One Player from Team A stands at one end of the gauntlet, one from Team B at the opposite end. They face each other. Everyone else stays in their lines, standing still with their heads bowed, making no sounds. The Players in the gauntlet make eye contact with each other: *they must hold it throughout the game.*

To start, they bow (still keeping eye contact), and as they bow, they say loudly, in unison: 'Ha-goo', finishing the word as they rise from the bow. They start walking towards one another at a slow, steady pace. When they meet in the middle, the pair turn a half-circle, still facing one another, so they are now walking backwards towards the opposite end of the gauntlet to where they started. When they get back to the end of the line, still maintaining eye contact, they bow again and say 'Ha-goo.'

Simple, eh? Well, once the Players finish saying 'Ha-goo' at the start, the teams are doing everything they can to make the Player from the opposing team laugh. Anything goes – including sounds, words, jokes, physical play, etc. But there are four rules:

- No team member can make physical contact with the Players in the gauntlet.

- They cannot block their view of their opponent for any length of time.

- They cannot impede the Players' forward progress.

- They cannot move down the line: they try to make the other team's Player laugh from their place in line.

This continues until the opponents bow and finish saying 'Ha-goo.'

A laugh – even the hint of a smile – will lose the game, as will either Player breaking eye contact with their opponent.

If a team gets the opposing Player to do any of these things, the Guide ends the match and gives each Player on the winner's team a treat, such as an M&M or other type of snack (have a mix for those who don't want sweets or can't have nuts). Once the snacks are handed out, two more Players step into the gauntlet and the game begins again.

+ M&Ms and other such small snacks

Skills
Competition, Ensemble Play, Improvisation

28

Fox and Squirrel

This is a good game to introduce tactics, strategies, ensemble collaboration and competition.

The Players stand in a circle, holding one large and one small ball (for large groups, have two large balls, or separate the group into two teams of at least ten Players). The Players stand close enough so they can pass balls left or right without throwing.

The large ball is *Fox*, the small ball is *Squirrel*. Fox can only be handed off to another Player to the left or right in either direction; it cannot be thrown across the circle. Squirrel can be passed left or right but can also be thrown across the circle.

When handing or throwing Squirrel to someone, the Players must call out the name of that person before they throw it.

The catching Player must catch it and call the name of someone else *before* throwing again; they cannot just hit it towards another Player.

The objective is to pass Fox left or right so that the Player with the Fox ball can use the ball to tag the body of the Player with Squirrel while the Squirrel ball is still in their hands. Play a few rounds to get the hang of it.

Add: When a Player holding Squirrel is tagged, they step out of the circle. As the group gets smaller, the play gets more intense. When playing with two Fox balls, take one out when nine Players remain.

Side-coaching

- Encourage the Players to play with time: pass Squirrel quickly, or hold it as they watch Fox get passed around. Fox cannot jump across the circle, so the Player holding Squirrel can wait to see which way around the circle Fox will go. They can wait until the last minute to throw Squirrel or toss it to someone close to Fox to get them tagged out.

- How do those with Fox collaborate to get Squirrel? How can they help Squirrel, to keep him from getting caught? What are the individual tactics? What are the group's strategies?

28

COMPETITION

+ Two volleyball-sized balls (Foxes) and one smaller ball (about 20cm diameter – Squirrel) of a different colour

Skills
Collaboration, Competition, Ensemble Play, Timing, Warm-Up

29

COMPETITION

Dragon's Jewels

This game is intense and fast-moving, great for getting everyone focused. It is also good for exploring individual tactics for winning and ensemble collaboration, including losing in order to help someone else win. Because it's a fast-paced game, there are many chances for a Player to explore their tactics for both success and failure.

Have groups of five Players working in different areas of the room. One Player is *Dragon*, kneeling on a mat, the other four are *Knights*. They stand in a circle around Dragon. A thick sock or a hand towel is placed on the mat; these are Dragon's jewels. Dragon kneels over them, his hands on the mat. He cannot sit on, hold or move the jewels.

Dragon strikes the mat to begin. Knights circle Dragon, trying to steal jewels from under him without getting tagged. If a Knight is tagged, she's frozen for the remainder of the game. Knight who gets the jewels becomes Dragon and the game starts again.

Knights can distract Dragon with movement, sounds, words or touch, as they circle Dragon and search for ways to reach in and snatch the jewels. Dragon uses his arms to sweep the space around him, or tries a series of quick tags, to get as many Knights as possible. If he tags all the Knights, he remains Dragon, and strikes the mat to begin again; the others unfreeze and make another attempt at getting the jewels.

Side-coaching

- What are each individual's strategies (physical and tactical) for getting the jewels and becoming Dragon?

- How does the group work together to distract Dragon so that one Knight can snatch the jewels?

- How does Dragon use his body to defend the jewels? What are his tactics for tagging Knights whilst protecting the jewels?

- Don't just focus on winning: a Player can sacrifice themselves so someone else can snatch the jewels. For example, a Knight can go for the jewels so that when they're tagged, their frozen body blocks Dragon's movement or sightlines, making it easier for the other Knights to snatch the jewels.
- The Players are encouraged to risk losing, play with tactics, to make the game a scene, not just a competition.

+ Thick socks or small towels, gym mats

Skills
Collaboration, Competition, Ensemble Play, Warm-Up

30 Snatch Tail

COMPETITION

This game emphasises tactics and making quick, physical decisions; it's also good for exploring a Player's relationship to winning and losing, and toying with both.

Duos: The Players form two lines facing each other with a three-metre gap between them. Each line spreads out so the aisle between the teams is nine metres long. Cover the playing area with gym mats as this game can get quite physical. Each Player has a sock tucked in the back of their waistband with two-thirds of the sock protruding like a tail.

The Guide calls out the names of two Players who enter the space between the lines and try to snatch each other's tail while protecting their own. They cannot hold or lie down on their tail, nor can they physically restrain their opponent. Once a tail is snatched out of a waistband, the Player who lost their tail returns to one of the lines. The Player who snatched the tail stays in and a new name is called.

Note: The Players in the lines on either side should be ready to keep the opponents in the playing area, physically catching them if necessary and easing them back in.

Trios: Same as above, but the Guide can call out a third name. A third Player can join forces with one of the others by shaking hands; then they gang up on the other Player. Or the Players already in the game join forces with a handshake. Or no one joins up and it's every Player for themselves.

If two Players who have teamed up grab the sock of the other Player, the duo then face off and try to snatch each other's tails. This happens as soon as the third Player loses his tail. The two remaining Players should stay on their guard: the Guide may still call another name.

Slow-Mo: Mark off a space with rope or gym mats laid on the floor, just large enough for the group to stand with a little more than an arm's length between each Player. Everyone moves in slow motion while trying to snatch each other's tails. Players are disqualified if they speed up. If a tail is snatched, that Player steps out of the area (in slow motion, of course).

Side-coaching

- Get physical with the snatching and protecting. Get acrobatic!

- Tease other Players with your tail, offer it as an easy target, dare them to snatch it… then let them take it. Or turn at the last minute and grab theirs. Develop tactics, find variety in the playing of the game, in how to win *and* lose, deliberately.

- Stay aware of the audience as the game is played. They're intimately involved in the game; even though they're on the sidelines, they're physically keeping the Players in the playing space and, at any moment, they may be called into the game. The line between Player and observer is thin.

- Each Player will get a number of turns, so they should see each turn as an opportunity to make a real connection with another Player, to make the play with their partner dynamic and engaging, not just competitive.

+ Socks, rope, gym mats

Skills

Collaboration, Competition, Duos, Ensemble Play, Trios

31 Snatch the Prize

This game has a good progression: each variation creates new possibilities for play and the need for greater focus. The Players have to think more about tactics and expand their awareness to take in more actions and more options.

Duos: The Players form two lines facing each other with a three-metre gap between them. Each line spreads out so the aisle between the teams is nine metres long. This is the playing area. A handkerchief or other soft prop is placed on the floor between the lines; this is the *prize*. The Guide calls a name from each line then says 'Go!' Each Player's objective is to snatch the prize and get back to their place in line before their opponent tags them. If they get back with the prize, the Guide places it back in the middle (or any place between the lines) and calls two new names (or calls one new name while the winner of last game goes again).

If the Player who grabs the prize is tagged before getting back in line, they set the prize on the floor where the tag happened. The two Players take three steps away from it, count to three in unison, and try again to grab it and return to their spot without getting tagged.

Trios: In this version, the Guide can call out another Player from either line; this is done at the start or while two Players are in the midst of playing. All try to grab the prize and tag each other, or two Players can work together – they make the decision to team up by shaking hands – and compete against the third Player. Or the Players who are already in the middle join forces and team up against the new Player. Once a pair of Players team up, they stay that way until someone gets the prize and gets back to their place in line.

If someone is tagged, they set the prize on the floor where the tag happened. All the Players take three steps away from it, count to three in unison, and try again to grab it and return to their spot without getting tagged.

Note: It's difficult for one person to win against two. Knowing they have this advantage, how does the duo play in such a way to make the game more interesting?

Prize Held: The Guide stands in the playing area and holds the prize in her outstretched hand. Names are called, the Guide says 'Go!' and the Players snatch the prize from the Guide. She can remain neutral – holding the prize until it's grabbed – or she can toy with the Players, holding the prize low or up high, or moving it out of reach at any moment. Once a Player gets the prize, he tries to get back in line before getting tagged. If he's tagged, the Guide holds the prize where the tag happened, all Players take three steps from it, count to three and start again.

The Guide holding the prize becomes an unpredictable element of the game. She can also call out a third Player at any time.

Side-coaching

- The Players make it a competition with one objective: grab the prize, get back to their position and win!
- The Players make it a scene: they play with time, approach the prize slowly, put all their attention on their opponent as they manoeuvre closer to the prize. They explore the physical, mental and emotional interaction between each other and how that plays to the audience. They delay, they tease, they risk losing in order to create greater tension and variety. How could this kind of play be applied to a scene?

+ A large handkerchief, tea towel, soft toy, hat, etc.
Skills
Collaboration, Competition, Duos, Improvisation, Trios

PART FIVE

COLLABORATION

*Exploring the dynamics of collaborating
(and collaborating while competing)*

The clown is a person at play in an expansive – not exaggerated – way. The clown is not a cartoon, but a person engaging with the world in an intensely curious, vigorously imaginative way. One of the best ways to expand a person's potential is through collaboration. Two or more minds, hearts, bodies and spirits working together towards a common objective, increases the potential of all involved if they listen and respond to what their partners offer.

As collaborators explore an exercise together, possibilities gather around them, invisible forces join them, sometimes encouraging synchronicity, other times creating mischief, tossing inspiring accidents their way. Working with their partners and these unseen forces, the Players uncover new ways to play a game, new possibilities for devising material, feeding ideas to each other through eye contact, breath, sound and movement.

Expanding the potential of a game, by toying with the rules and finding variations, teaches the Players how to do the same to a devised routine or scene. They learn to listen not just with their ears, but their entire body. Through collaboration, they develop an expanded awareness, enabling them to tune in to their partners on a deeper level. This continues and intensifies the work done earlier with **Energy** (Part One).

Collaborative games show how group energy influences individuals and vice versa. The Players work as a chorus but also support each other's solo moments. They follow the prompts of a leader but are also able to influence the leader's actions.

Pressure Points

This is a playful exploration between the Players, their movements and objects. It's a good 'physical listening' game.

Ball, Palm, Body: Four or more Players, each with a round beanbag, tennis ball or balled-up newspaper wrapped in masking tape, surround another Player who is *Leader*. The Players press their object against some part of Leader's body with an open hand; each Player chooses a different place. They experiment with where the object is placed: the top of the foot, the back of the knee, the side of the head, under the arm, etc. When all Players have made contact, the Guide plays some music (something lyrical, not too strong a beat), and Leader starts to move; the Players move with him, trying to keep their objects from falling, their only point of contact is their open hand pressing their object against Leader's body (they cannot switch hands). If an object is dropped, the Player who dropped it picks it up and steps out of the game. The range and speed of movement can increase as Players drop out, but the objective is for Leader to maintain contact with the Players via the objects.

The Derry Variation: Same as above, but the Players can apply pressure to the object, making Leader more aware of each point of contact, sometimes pushing him, forcing him to move in the direction of the push. Leader can go with this force or push back. The Players shouldn't overdo it; they make a choice now and then to apply pressure and influence Leader's movement, staying aware of how Leader moves and what the other Players are doing.

Add: Try it with Leader blindfolded.

> **+ Round beanbags, tennis balls or newspaper balls wrapped in masking tape, music player and playlist, blindfold**
>
> **Skills**
> *Collaboration, Ensemble Play, Following, Improvisation, Leading, Listening*

Dance and Get Off the Floor

33

This is a fun, physical game that combines both competition and collaboration.

This game can be played with groups of four playing in different areas of the room. The Guide sets four chairs in a circle; there should be one less chair than the number of Players, and one chair must be strong enough to take the weight of all four Players. A lounge chair, sturdy wooden boxes or short, low benches could also be used, one Player per seat.

The Guide plays music. The Players dance around the chairs. When the music stops, everyone sits. The Player that doesn't get a chair needs to get her feet off the ground by, for example, sitting on someone's lap, standing on a chair occupied by someone else, laying across the laps of more than one Player, etc. The Guide removes a chair and the Players repeat the sequence. In the end, all the Players have to find a way to be off the ground, clinging to each other on a single chair.

Note: This kind of play could easily be used in an act or scene: the Players are commanded to sit but there aren't enough chairs onstage. They madly scramble for the chairs and find inventive ways to all sit, creating eccentric physical and visual tableaux.

+ Strong chairs, music player and playlist

Skills
Collaboration, Competition, Timing, Trust

34 Body Hide

This game will get the Players cooperating physically and get those observing involved in challenging and collaborating with those onstage.

Four-Hiding-One: Stage flats (or curtains) are set on either side of gym mats covering an area approximately 3x4 metres. Five Players enter from behind the flats and face the audience.

The Guide calls the name of one Player. The other four try and hide her using only their bodies. The audience call out whatever body part they can still see: 'Foot! Head! Shoulder!' When the Player's body is completely hidden (they may all be on the floor by this point), the Guide calls out 'Exit!'

The Players leave, keeping the hidden Player obscured until all are offstage. As they exit, the audience continues to call out what they can see.

Hide-or-Be-Seen: In this variation, the Player who is being hidden turns it into a game of hide-or-be-seen: sometimes he lets himself be hidden, sometimes he sticks a hand out, a leg, pops his head up, etc. The Guide calls 'Exit!' The group leaves, trying to keep the Player hidden until all are offstage. He keeps playing hide-or-be-seen as they exit.

The Player being hidden should play with time, staying hidden for long moments, then appearing; or popping up repeatedly then disappearing for a time; or being obvious about being seen; or being subtle, *sneaking* a leg into view, enjoying the play with the audience.

Note: This is a physically playful way for clowns to enter and/or exit a scene, or for a solo clown to be revealed from within a group or hidden from the audience. The game itself plays like a clown routine.

Side-coaching

- The Players work out a strategy with their partners *physically*, they don't discuss it.

- The Players must keep aware of the scope of the audience's view. Don't just block in the front: be mindful of what can be seen from the sides.

COLLABORATION

+ Gym mats to cover an area approximately 3x4 metres, curtains or stage flats
Skills
Collaboration, Competition, Ensemble Play, Improvisation

35 Snake Pit

Even though there is a competition between Snake and Mouse in this game, all Players collaborate on a number of levels. It's another game played with eyes covered, so it helps develop the other senses.

Ten or more Players form a circle holding hands (if the group is small, the Players can hold long towels or scarves between them to create a bigger playing area). Two Players are blindfolded; one Player is *Snake*, one is *Mouse*. Each gets a rattle – a plastic egg with grains in it works best, the two halves taped together. Don't use a maraca or plastic rattle with a handle as it may cause injury when Snake grabs Mouse.

Snake hunts Mouse by listening for movement, reaching out with her hands, or using her rattle: when she shakes it, Mouse must respond with a rattle of his own. Snake can only rattle three times (the group keeps count).

The group assists both Snake and Mouse by hissing when they get close to each other; the closer they get the louder the group hisses! The group can change the shape of the circle by moving in or out, or by forming different shapes, so long as they don't block Snake or Mouse from moving. After Snake's third rattle, the group counts out loud down from ten.

To win, Snake must find and hug Mouse before the group finishes counting. If she doesn't, Mouse wins. If Snake gets Mouse, Snake stays in the circle and a new Mouse is chosen. If Mouse wins, a new Snake is chosen.

Side-coaching

- What are the strategies for Mouse or Snake? How does each work with the disadvantage of being blindfolded? How does Snake use her rattle to trap Mouse? How does Mouse use his rattle to confuse Snake?
- How well does Snake listen in order to find Mouse? How does Mouse use listening (and stillness) to avoid getting caught?

- The Players should take note of the strategies of others and use them when they play Snake or Mouse.
- Move and think like a Snake or Mouse: small, subtle, always listening. Avoid large, fast or sharp movements until it's time to strike or escape.

+ Two blindfolds, three or more scarves or long towels, two rattles

Skills
Breath Work, Clarity, Competition, Duos, Ensemble Play, Improvisation, Listening, Timing

36 Orkestra

A good game for playing with group sound and movement. It helps bond the ensemble through vocal play and improvisation, and can be developed into a comedy routine.

Circle Sounds: The Players form a circle. The Guide starts a sound – this can be vocal or a percussive sound made with the body – maintaining its volume and rhythm. The Player to her right introduces a new sound. This continues around the circle, with each Player maintaining their sound until everyone has joined in and is contributing to the song; some Players may take the lead when they feel the urge. A Player can move closer to another Player who might have a similar sound or rhythm and try to develop their sounds together, all the while keeping their sounds connected to the entire Orkestra. The Guide will make a signal to end it, pointing at the Players one at a time to bring their sound to a close until all are silent.

Try with different styles of music and sound: funk, classical, jazz, absurd sounds, beatbox, etc.

Rehearsal: The Players form groups of six or more, comprising five or more *Musicians*, and one *Conductor* with a baton. Each Musician chooses a sound to make with their mouth – something they can hold for a few moments, or a brief blurt. The groups choose a tune to play, keeping it simple to start with, for example, 'Mary Had a Little Lamb'.

The groups are given time to rehearse and learn baton moves. For example, Conductor extending her arm and pointing the baton at a Musician means the Musician should sing and hold the note; bringing her arm back towards her chest means stopping; raising the baton high means a higher note; taking it low means a low note; pointing the baton at a Musician without pulling back means a solo for the Musician, who keeps singing the note while Conductor points to others with a finger and gets all the Musicians backing up the solo Musician; holding both arms straight out from the shoulders and raising them increases the group volume; bringing both arms down, lowers it; a slash sideways cuts off everyone.

Each group invents their own moves but shouldn't get too obsessive about getting them all perfect – it's more important to play with the sounds and use the awkwardness of missed cues or misunderstood baton moves to generate comedy and create status-play between Conductor and Musicians.

Performance: The first group to perform enters to applause. Musicians face the audience, Conductor has her back to them. Conductor points to each Musician to hear their sound and tries to get them all in tune. They begin on a cue from Conductor: she uses her baton to create the song, find variations, etc. Conductor's job is to set the rhythm and the time for each note (long or short). Musicians must remember the tune and their sound in order to add to the melody and follow Conductor's lead to play the tune.

Side-coaching

- Listen to each sound that is made to know when and how to add more sounds to increase the play and the vocal possibilities. How does each Player alter their sound to better fit into and add to the whole?

- Find harmony within the group, both in sound and in the reactions to each other. Once this is established, play with disharmony, coming in at the wrong time, too loud or too soft, missing a cue, etc., while keeping the tune going.

+ Stage flats or curtains, sticks

Skills
Clarity, Collaboration, Devising, Ensemble Play, Following, Improvisation, Leading, Listening, Timing

Who Started It?

A game that requires individual concentration and group focus, and the ability to pay attention to many things all going on at once.

The Players sit in a circle. One is chosen to be *Observer* and leaves the room while the others choose a *Leader*. Observer returns to the centre of the circle. Leader starts a game – it can be waving a hand or raising an eyebrow. The Players copy Leader and continue the movement until she changes it.

The objective is for the Players not to reveal to Observer who Leader is, while Leader must change the game without getting caught by Observer, who must guess who's leading. If Observer guesses wrong, he must perform: the Guide makes him imitate a chicken, do three push-ups, sing a short verse from a nursery rhyme in falsetto, etc. When Observer guesses correctly, he joins the circle, a new Observer is chosen and leaves the room, the group chooses a new Leader, and the game starts again.

Side-coaching

- The Players work together to develop a variety of tactics for hiding Leader. How do they use these tactics to fool and misdirect Observer?

- The Players should try looking at the group rather than Leader to see when the game changes.

- As Observer, what are the tactics for finding Leader?

Skills
Collaboration, Competition, Ensemble Play, Following, Leading, Timing

PART SIX

PROVOCATION

Developing physical and mental flexibility with help from partners and the audience

Many people think of provocation as a negative thing. The dictionary defines it as 'action or speech that makes someone angry, especially deliberately'. A provocation questions our habits, knocks us out of our comfort zone, gets past our defences and under our skin. It demands our full attention.

A provocation from a clown can be bold – they come right out and throw the ball at the audience! Or it can start quietly, the clown hinting, offering the ball timidly. Or it can be a mix, the clown teasing, playing with the throw-and-catch, the give-and-take.

Clowns follow the rules at the outset, play the game as it's meant to be played, establish its parameters, its structure. But their play threatens to undermine the game through provocation, disrupting its form, pushing everyone to go further, look deeper. Not deliberately, but because their curiosity and their imagination spur them on.

Provocation seeks to develop a Player's physical and mental flexibility, extends their understanding of tactics, strategies, bending and breaking rules, and expands the scope of their play.

38 The Audience: Yay! Boo!

PROVOCATION

In this exercise, the Players explore their reactions to an audience that is with them, and one that is against them. They learn how to toy with a vocally demanding audience (demanding more play, or demanding they get off the stage).

Yay! Boo!: Two Players wait backstage. The Guide shows two signals to the audience: a thumbs-up means they all cheer 'Yay!' and applaud for the one who enters; a thumbs-down means they all 'Boo!' at them.

The first Player enters; the audience cheers or boos according to the signal given previously by the Guide. The Player onstage reacts however they wish to the 'Yay!' or 'Boo!' It might scare them, make them sad, they might taunt the audience, ask them to be more vocal in their disapproval, or louder in their approval. Maybe they're confused by the crowd's reaction…

The audience toys with the Player's reaction by cheering or booing louder or more vehemently, but they stay with what the Guide signals throughout the Player's time onstage. The Guide cues the Player to exit, or they can exit on their own. She gives a signal to the audience and the next Player enters.

The Guide can also give a thumbs-up or -down while a Player is onstage, changing the 'Yay!' or 'Boo!' at any moment.

+ Stage flats or curtains

Skills
Competition, Improvisation, Listening, Physical Expression, Solos

Nice and Nasty

A great game for exploring simplicity in partner play, and how to share moments with the audience.

The Players stand in a circle. The first Player turns left and does something nice to the next Player using only the face and body – a big smile, a hug, etc. The second Player reacts, shows his reaction to everyone in the circle (the audience), then changes his face and body: this transition moment (showing the expression on his face and body) sets up that he's going to do something *nasty* to the next Player. He does something nasty – pinching their arm, growling at them, making an ugly face, etc. That Player reacts, turns and shows her reaction to the audience, then changes her face and body *for the audience*: this transition moment sets up that she's going to do something *nice* to the next Player. This continues around the circle, alternately nice and nasty.

Note: These simple exchanges can be very funny to do and observe. Part of the enjoyment is the moment of transition and the anticipation it sets up as to what will happen next. In physical comedy, understanding and utilising moments of transition – and sharing them with the audience – is crucial to communicating ideas and emotions, and creating a stronger connection.

Side-coaching

- The Players should make each beat clear, to fully engage with their partners and with everyone in the circle on the transitions.

- Share the transition moment with them *before* the action, to build up anticipation.

- Be eccentric, weird, playful, goofy, lyrical, etc. The Players should be encouraged to explore sounds and movements that surprise their audience and their partners, to go outside their comfort zone (and to provoke others to do the same!).

Skills
Clarity, Collaboration, Devising, Duos, Listening, Physical Expression
---

The Provocateur

40

PROVOCATION

This exercise can help the Players get comfortable with being interrupted – forgetting a line, a rehearsed action in a scene, the progression of their well-planned act, etc., and spur creative ways to play with interruptions.

Preparation for Say Yes: Individually, Players develop an act or scene (using vocal sounds is alright but no words), keeping it one minute or less. It can be a juggling trick, a cartwheel, standing on one leg, sitting on a chair, folding a dress, wiping something off the floor with a rag, etc. They rehearse it until they know each action so well that it is easily repeatable.

Say Yes: A Player has come to audition their act or scene. They make an entrance, move downstage and perform the act. The Guide asks them to do it again – starting with the entrance – and as they do, the Guide begins to comment on the act. Whatever the Guide says, the Player says yes (this can be vocalised with a sound or simply a nod); for example, the Guide might say: 'Your act isn't very good' and the Player agrees and tries again; or 'Your costume is on wrong' and the Player adjusts it. This continues until the Guide tells the Player to exit.

Note: The objective is for the Player to hear the comments, agree with them, adjust, then try again to see what sort of play and invention occurs.

The Player should tune in to how the audience responds to the Guide's challenges and their reactions; how can the solo Player win over the crowd by using the challenges?

Preparation for Yes, Tic, Wind-Up: The Players find a physical *Tic* – like an electric shock that causes some part of their body to twitch, spasm or jerk – and a physicalised preparation – a *Wind-Up* – such as shaking out the arms, hopping straight up in the air, stretching the body, etc. – before executing their act. The Tic and the Wind-Up can be almost anything that's short and easily repeatable (see Game 54: *Wind-Up, Stall, Repeat, Breathe*).

Yes, Tic, Wind-Up: The Player makes an entrance, moves downstage and performs his act as above, but every time the Guide says the Player's name, he Tics, and every time the Guide says 'Go' the Player does his Wind-Up before doing the act. The Guide should challenge the Player, timing the cues for the Tic and the Wind-Up to push the Player's act into the absurd, getting them off-balance in order to generate new ideas and expand the possibilities for play.

Note: The moments prior to the main act or scene – the Set-Up – are the best time to express and share the clown with the audience. The interruptions and physical reactions can be developed to reveal the Player's emotions and state of mind. This is explored further in Game 59: The Set-Up and the Scene.

Side-coaching

- The provocations and interruptions will disrupt the Players' train of thought and action, leaving them a bit flustered; saying Yes, and playing with the Tic and Wind-Up will give them breathing space – a chance to delay the usual drive towards getting to the big act – and instead will help them explore ways of tweaking the presentation around the trick: building interest and suspense, and revealing the clown.

- It's important to be able to perform an act while responding to outside stimuli, turn interruptions into opportunities, learn to work them into an act so what was a troublesome disruption becomes a playful, comic moment – a part of the performance and of an act's evolution.

+ Stage flats or curtains, any props needed for the scenes
Skills
Devising, Following, Improvisation, Listening, Physical Expression, Solos, Timing

41

In and Out – But Only Two

This feels like the beginning of a scene, but it can also play like a game of Chase and Tag *(Game 15). The Players should keep both in mind: come out to play for the audience but remember to abide by the rules of the game.*

Only Two: Three Players wait backstage. Two enter: they can improvise most anything but must be ready to exit when the third Player enters; someone *must* leave as there can only be two people onstage at any time. The third Player can enter and exit immediately, or the other two onstage can negotiate which of them will exit. The Players should turn the entrances and exits into a game, and explore the improvised play that happens while adhering to the rule that only two people can be onstage at any time. The Guide should reprimand the Players any time there are more than two of them onstage.

Add: Start with four or more Players backstage. Increase the number of Players allowed onstage to three. This one can get a bit crazy!

Scene: Five or more Players wait backstage. Decide on a setting and how many Players are onstage at any time; for example, how many are visible for a party, a funeral, a doctor's waiting room, a busy restaurant? Along with the guests, patients, attendees, or customers, include the host, a pizza-delivery guy, the undertaker(s), the doctor(s), the chef, waiter, busboy, etc. Enact the scene while playing the game of *In and Out – But Only Three* (or *Four* or *Five*…) to develop the action and the scene.

Keep playing the game as it develops into a scene without making the rules obvious. For example, a Player could rush off suddenly then explain why when they return. Or they could apologise, find an excuse as to why they must leave again before going. A Player could suddenly remember there's something they forgot in another room of the house, leave to look for a coffin, to talk to the

PROVOCATION

nurse, to get something from the kitchen. They could pretend to hear someone calling them from another room, etc.

Play the game and the scene and find an ending where all exit, or the Guide signals to the Players to finish the scene.

PROVOCATION

+ Stage flats or curtains, any props needed for the scenes

Skills
Collaboration, Competition, Devising, Ensemble Play, Improvisation, Listening

Pop Goes the Beastie

This is a rambunctious game that always brings out the playful 'beastie' in the Players, allowing them to experience – on a visceral level – the play of the ensemble and the tension between wanting to go their own way and wanting to belong to the group. A good way to bring out another level of play and a different approach to clowning that gravitates toward the style of performing known as 'bouffon'.

Note: Players should be instructed to wear underwear and loose-fitting clothing that has some stretch to it.

The Players blow up balloons and place them in a large box or bin bags so they are ready for the game (three balloons for each Player, in groups of five). A large, thick gym mat or a stack of mattresses about half a metre high are placed in the centre of the room. This is the throne for Big Beastie. Using a large cardboard box or other square barrier, create another container for the balloons to be placed downstage-right or -left of the throne. Put in enough so each Player has three. The Guide tells the Players they must stick to their quota of three balloons per Beastie.

The group is divided into packs of five Beasties per pack. The first pack lies on the floor with eyes closed, away from the throne and balloons. Beasties go to sleep. They make sounds, dream Beastie dreams, as the rest of the group watches…

The Guide hits a drum and the Beasties take their time waking up, assuming this creature and finding its physicality (Beasties are a cross between an ape, a pig, a hyena and a chicken). They acknowledge the pack and their relationships to each other as they groom themselves, tussle, stretch, and wake up. The Guide gives the Players time to explore and become a Beastie.

As a pack, the Beasties see the balloons, move to them and begin to stuff them into their clothes (only three per Beastie). The balloons give them energy; as the Beasties stuff their clothes, they become animated, stronger, more Beastie-like.

They might choose to stuff a balloon into the clothes of other Beasties in the pack, enjoying the sharing and feeding. Or squabbles may happen, balloons may pop; if so, some Beasties will end up with less than their quota. When all the balloons are stuffed in their clothes, the Beasties roar and show off, eager to prove they are the biggest Beastie!

At some point one of the Beasties sees the throne and decides to climb on it. The problem is, every Beastie wants to sit on the throne and be the Big Beastie. Scuffles break out, Beasties argue, make Beastie sounds. They know that if they pop another Beastie's balloons it weakens them; if they pop them all, it will kill them. The inner struggle for each Beastie is the tension between wanting to be the Big Beastie sitting on the throne ruling over everyone, but wanting also to be part of the pack, to belong to the group – a Beastie needs his pack to survive! But the throne beckons…

Balloons will end up popping for different reasons: while Beasties fight over the throne, while they wrestle or groom each other; maybe they pop them out of curiosity, jealousy, playfulness, by accident, or deliberately in order to take out another Beastie. Each pop elicits a reaction from both Beasties and the pack. Balloons may fall out of a Beastie's clothes – other Beasties may pick them up and stuff them into their own clothes, offer them back, or pop them!

As their balloons are popped, a Beastie loses energy. When all a Beastie's balloons are popped, she crawls away from the pack to die. The scene continues until there is only one Beastie left, sitting on the throne. BIG BEASTIE RULES! But Big Beastie is now alone; the pack has all died…

The Guide then hits the drum to end the scene.

Note: The Guide can keep a club handy (a foam pool noodle or pipe insulation) to corral Beasties or provoke them, reminding them to react as a Beastie and not in a human way. Foam bat in hand, the Guide acts the part of the almighty Boss Beastie.

PROVOCATION

Side-coaching

- The Players explore the tension of the conflicting objectives: protecting their balloons, while popping and taking out other Beasties in order to be Big Beastie, the one on the throne; but also wanting to be part of a pack for protection, affection and camaraderie.

- The Players should be encouraged to keep discovering and exploring their inner Beastie throughout the scene: how do they act in a pack; how do they serve their own interests; how can they feed the group as well as their own Beastie ego?

+ Gym mats, balloons, boxes/bin liners, a drum, a foam bat

Skills
Collaboration, Competition, Ensemble Play, Improvisation, minimum-to-MAXIMUM, Status

PART SEVEN

COMPLICATION

Using restrictions, problems and accidents to generate material

It's hard to fake a problem: everyone knows that embarrassing, sometimes painful feeling of things going wrong and others witnessing your discomfort. They know this on a *visceral* level, so they can easily detect when a clown is faking a problem. One of the hardest things to pull off in clowning is that wide-eyed naivety, the sense that you are truly baffled by a situation.

One way to help the Players understand and express this feeling of bafflement is to create a real obstacle that limits their ability to perceive a situation, or disadvantages them physically (e.g. a blindfold or restricting the use of their hands by always keeping them in their pockets). When a Player experiences a real obstacle as they play a scene, they understand on a gut level what it means to be flummoxed.

Many of the best comic bits are revealed by complications during the development process. In my own work, at least thirty per cent or more of the material in my shows came about when a genuine problem occurred while improvising or rehearsing, and I dived in and explored it rather than avoided it. Or something did not go according to plan in the midst of a performance and I didn't freeze but played with the problem; the audience applauded my cleverness (or luck). I experienced two powerful emotions: the terror of things going wrong, followed by the thrill of turning it into an opportunity, hearing the crowd's laughter and seeing my show expand.

When the Players learn to turn problems into possibilities, they begin to actively look for ways to create obstacles for themselves! They gain confidence, knowing that whatever happens they can play with it. Taking a problem and turning it into an advantage is one of the essential survival and performance skills of a clown; it generates empathy between the clown and their audience, allowing them to share in an experience that we all know and are affected by deeply. The audience will applaud the clown's resilience, fortitude, resourcefulness, imagination – and luck!

43 The Invaders

COMPLICATION

I developed this exercise while working at Shakespeare's Globe, London. The female characters had to find ways to escape the advances of some of the male characters (and other females). It got the Players moving and interacting, while creating playful ways to respond to, accept or avoid contact.

In Your Space: The Players pair up; one is *Invader*, the other, *Responder*. They stand a metre or so apart at first. Then Invader steps in close to Responder in a way that makes him uncomfortable. Responder can *tolerate*: remain where he is, expressing how uncomfortable Invader's proximity makes him feel through facial expressions or small movements. Responder can *contract*: draw his head back, collapse or contract inwards, bend or twist in the spine. Responder can *deflect*: stepping back or sideways – the expression of discomfort is more obvious. Responder can *accept*: he doesn't move away but accepts the closeness – he may even step in closer. The Players explore the timing of the invasion and the response: is it drawn out or is it a quick move in and a quick move away? They then try again with a different invasion and response.

Both the Players explore various energies as Invader and Responder: they could be aggressive, coy, giddy, paranoid, confused, etc. They can try different physical tactics: as Invader, they can step up to Responder from the side, come up from behind and look over their shoulder, come in close and just stare at their ear, etc.; whilst Responder can squirm away, scream and jump, drop to the floor and crawl away, hug Invader awkwardly, overwhelm them with their response, etc.

Both the Players should take it easy at first; Invaders shouldn't lunge after Responder and risk losing their balance or knocking heads; they should keep any hugs or grips loose enough – or so telegraphed – that Responder (and audience) sees it coming, and they can break away from, duck out of, or block Invader's attempts. Once the Players are comfortable with the exercise, they can get more physical – even acrobatic! – as they make greater efforts to capture and escape, always keeping safety in mind and staying sensitive to their partner's responses.

Note: Responder can also welcome Invader, show that they want to be approached. They could overreact when Invader steps in close, grabbing and hugging them vigorously, turning the tables on them.

Scene: Develop a short scene: the Players make an entrance, play the game of invading and responding. The physical interaction can be flirtatious or irritating, but it can also be one Player trying to grab or hold on to the other Player to keep them close, stop them from moving about, get them to focus on what's happening, or listen to what their partner has to say; it doesn't have to involve flirtation or encroachment. The Players devise an exit, or the Guide signals them to finish the scene.

Side-coaching

- As Responders, the Players should first take time to discover what their honest, *real* reaction is to having their space invaded. Then explore other possibilities – in particular, the opposite of their natural reaction. For example, if a Player doesn't like people so close, they could step in closer when Invader gets in their space, and see how that affects their body and movement choices.

- The Guide should encourage the Players to work with stillness and slowed reactions. Imagine they're in a social situation; for example, they feel uncomfortable but they can't show it in an obvious way because this person is important to their career.

+ Stage flats or curtains, set pieces for the scene
Skills
Competition, Devising, Duos, Following, Improvisation, Leading, Status, Timing, Trust

Task and Time

This exercise always generates ideas for comic play. The speed – sometimes panic – that occurs when the Players are asked to play a scene faster, keeps them from overthinking their actions and reactions, and gives them ideas on how to edit and clarify – as well as expand on – simple tasks.

Preparation: The Players partner up and decide on a task they'll perform: folding bedsheets and blankets, stuffing pillows into pillowcases, stacking everything up, etc. Or they can bring a table onstage, cover it with a tablecloth, lay out cups and pour water into the cups. Or they can arrange the pages of a newspaper, the promotional flyers and supplements. They keep the scene no longer than two minutes.

Whatever the Players decide, it should involve props that can be treated (potentially) roughly; they should have no sharp edges and it shouldn't matter if they're torn, crushed or trashed, etc.

The Players rehearse the task a few times including an entrance and an exit. They run it without embellishing or trying to make it funny, enacting only the necessary actions that accomplish the task.

Task and Time: The duo can choose to enter with their props or have them already set onstage. They run through the task at normal speed and exit, while the Guide times them from the moment they enter until they leave the stage. The duo then repeats the scene but with the Guide shaving off fifteen seconds. So, if it took one minute initially, they must now do it in forty-five seconds. They then repeat it but in thirty seconds. Then fifteen. Then the Guide shaves off five seconds, so the Players do the scene in ten seconds. The Players should try to do all actions even with the time reduced. If this is impossible, they can edit, hitting the high points of the scene (see Game 63: *Seven Snapshots* for ways to do this).

Note: Timing is all important in comedy. An exercise like this makes the Players acutely aware of this, forcing them to grapple with and learn to enjoy, changes in pace, rhythm and time. This exercise can be used with most any act or scene.

Side-coaching

- To keep from stressing about losing time, the Players should focus on their partners, go with whatever comes up between them.
- Losing time forces the Players to think on their feet. The body – in action – may discover something the brain would never have thought of.

+ Stage flats or curtains, props

Skills
Collaboration, Devising, Duos, Improvisation, Timing

The Eyes Have It: The Trick

This exercise uses the same technique as Game 26: The Eyes Have It: Choices to create obstacles that challenge the Players to find different ways to connect with an audience. This version has them adding a simple action with a prop.

Preparation: The Players develop a short act with one of two prop choices: a stiff felt hat or a ball. They're given time to rehearse an entrance, moving to where they will present the act – it must involve throwing the hat or ball in the air and catching it, with the hat ending up placed on the head, the ball held under an arm – they then make an exit with the prop. They rehearse this sequence and the trick until they can do it smoothly and comfortably, without embellishing.

Never Look: Three Players wait backstage. One Player enters, moves to a spot anywhere onstage, presents their trick, then exits. During this sequence he *never makes eye contact with the audience* from the moment he enters until he exits. As soon as he exits, another Player enters, does their trick and exits, never making eye contact. The third Player enters as soon as the second Player exits and does the same.

Note: As soon as a Player exits, the next one enters – but no sooner; the Guide should call out anyone who stalls in the entrance or comes out before the other Player is completely offstage.

Always Look: Same as above, but the Players *always make eye contact with the audience* – from the moment they enter, *while they are doing the trick*, and until they are completely offstage. The Guide should call out any moments a Player looks away, usually while trying to catch the thrown hat or ball. If they do look away even for a moment, the Guide makes them repeat the scene until they can do it, always looking at the audience. The next Player enters as soon as they exit and plays their scene, and so on.

Choose Your Moment: Same as above, but the Players choose to make eye contact with the audience only once at any moment in the sequence. It can be as soon as they enter, before, during or after the trick, or just before they exit. Only one short look is allowed, not a prolonged staring out.

Note: Clowns are always eager to connect with their crowd and the eyes are one of the most effective ways to do this. In the second variation, this eagerness – manifested by always looking to the audience – can lead to some great comic play!

Side-coaching

- Adding any action(s) to the technique of using the eyes in different ways to connect with an audience, immediately alters the dynamic of the relationship between the Player and the public, the Player and the object, and the Player and their actions.

- Take note of how the different ways to use the eyes – in a conscious way – can connect the audience and the Player, and how this can be used in a routine or scene.

+ Stage flats or curtains, thick, stiff felt hats, different-sized balls

Skills
Clarity, Collaboration, Improvisation, Physical Expression, Solos, Timing

46

COMPLICATION

The Variation

In this exercise, Players expand the possibilities of a single action to find more variety in their play.

Preparation: The Players are given time to find variations on any actions they execute in a routine or scene. For example, if a Player's action was throwing a ball in the air and catching it, she might try throwing it up with the back of her hand, from the crook of her elbow, off the top of her foot, etc. She wouldn't put in a pirouette as that would be *adding* to the action. What is needed is a variation on the action of throwing that makes it more interesting, eccentric or skilful. The Players should look for as many variations on each action as possible within an allotted rehearsal time.

The Variation: A Player enters and presents her scene. At any point, the Guide can say 'Variation.' Whatever the Player is doing, at that prompt she shows a variation of the action, then continues as before. The Guide may then let her carry on with the scene or ask for another variation on the same action.

This is a good technique to use in rehearsals. Once the Players run through a scene, they look for variations on their actions, especially ones that are done in a pedestrian way: taking off a coat and hat, hanging them up, opening a suitcase, taking things out, setting chairs around a table, etc.

Note: Variations are when the playful mind really starts to reveal and stretch itself! Taking an everyday action and doing it in an eccentric way is one of the hallmarks of clowning.

Side-coaching

- Players shouldn't let the request for variations fluster them but see them as opportunities to develop the details of a scene, and find playful ways to do mundane actions.
- Know the difference between a variation and an addition; moving to an addition too soon risks

losing an opportunity for imaginative play, a chance to explore the possibilities of a single action.

- Searching for variations is a useful way to generate new ideas, expand and draw focus to a moment, and to build up a backlog of ideas that can be used when improvising.

+ Stage flats or curtains, various props

Skills
Devising, Improvisation, Listening, Physical Expression, Solos

47 Incoming!

I have used this not only as an exercise in itself, but as a way to liven up or provoke the Players in almost any scene, improvised, devised or scripted. It keeps the Players aware of the world outside a scene, and encourages them to incorporate and play with other realities that may invade their performance.

Preparation: Players partner up. They can perform acts or scenes created in earlier exercises, or develop new ones, keeping things short and simple. The Players can use props or not. If using props, they can't use more than two.

The Guide has a collection of props close at hand and stands by the stage. The props must all be objects that are durable, so they can be tossed or rolled onto the stage – balls, stuffed toys, blankets, newspapers, tennis raquets, metal bowls, plastic buckets, etc.

Incoming: Two Players enter and begin their act or scene. At any point, the Guide may toss or roll a prop onto the stage. The Players decide if they will incorporate it into the task, or simply see it and carry on. They don't have to use it right away (they may find a moment later on in their scene to include it), but they must see it or show they are aware of it in some way (a shift in their posture, a change in the rhythm of the scene, one Player laughing nervously, etc.).

The Guide can throw more props onto the stage or let the Players carry on with only the one offered. The Players end the scene on their own or the Guide tells them to finish and exit.

Note: The interventions by the props can stimulate play. They can also open up a scene that becomes too internal, where partners aren't playing with each other, or connecting with the crowd; or it can be used to stir up some creative chaos.

+ Stage flats or curtains, various props

Skills
Devising, Duos, Following, Improvisation, Listening, Prop Play, Timing, Trios

PART EIGHT

IMPROPISATION

Using props to reveal thoughts, emotions, develop relationships and devise material

Clowns use props to reveal thoughts and emotions, develop relationships, and tell stories. Through their imaginative play, any object – ball, coat, juggling clubs, microphone, Jester's head on a stick, guitar, mop – has the potential to be transformed into a partner.

A chair becomes an obstacle for a clown to trip over or struggle to sit on, an adversary that antagonises the clown. It can also be a metaphor for what a clown is struggling with internally.

In order to bring a prop to life, to expand its potential, a Player must spend time with it, get to know what it's capable of, and listen to its ideas. A prop will play with them just as another Player would if they learn how to listen to it: an object talks via its texture, its shape, the sounds it makes when interacted with, what it does when it's lifted, thrown, rolled, dropped, or the ways it can be transformed into something else. The more time spent playing with an object, the more it will suggest, the more imaginative the play with this prop partner can be.

Good technique (especially manipulation techniques, like those used in puppetry) and a lively imagination are paramount. If these skills are developed in relation to objects, then Players will never lack for partners. They can walk into any space with the knowledge that something will offer itself, and they'll experience the pleasure an audience gets out of seeing an object they often pay no attention to suddenly come alive and become a partner in the play.

Working with props requires the same kind of dedicated practice as learning any skill, such as juggling (handling and focusing on many things at once), magic (misdirection), and acrobatics (slapstick with props). For prop masters, see Buster Keaton, W. C. Fields, Jacques Tati, Lucille Ball, Tim Conway, Slava Polunin, Rowan Atkinson as Mr Bean, Nola Rae, Philippe Genty, Yann Frisch, to name just a few.

Object Leads

In this exercise the Players use an object to help connect with their partners and introduce them to the possibilities for ensemble play via a prop.

The Players divide into groups of four. The Guide lays objects on the floor (for example, a bamboo cane, a large ball, a coat hanger, a paper cup, a cardboard box). Each group circles around an object. The Players make eye contact, breathe together, then squat down. Each Player takes hold of the object using only one finger, all making contact with it simultaneously; they then lift the object together.

Groups play with speed and shape, lifting the object high, taking it low, moving it sideways. They can sit with the object, lie down with it, or some can sit while others stand. The Players can treat their interaction like a dance, or work the object like a puppet. The Players should use the object, eye contact and breathing to stay connected to each other. Always ensure that everyone can maintain contact with the object using only one finger each.

The Guide calls an end to the exercise. The Players lay the object down, all letting go at the same time. They stand, make eye contact and breathe together. The groups then try again with a different object. Also try mixing up the members of the groups. Each prop encourages its own way of communicating, so offer a variety – but avoid objects with lots of parts or sharp edges, or ones that are too soft for the group to manipulate.

Note: If an object falls, the Players in the group should stop and lift the object together as they did at the start. This exercise is about prop play, but also about ensemble connection. When that connection is broken, the Players should take a moment to reconnect before carrying on.

+ Various props

Skills
Breath Work, Collaboration, Ensemble Play, Improvisation, Introductions, Prop Play

Props-Go-Round

There is a lot going on in this exercise! It's ensemble play and prop manipulation with multiple objects, but also a memory game and a competitive sport.

The Guide assembles different props, for example: a hat, a volleyball, a half-metre-long stick, a juggling ring or small hoop that fits over the head, a thick book. The Players form groups of seven and stand in a circle. Each object must be passed in a different way and in a set order, for example: the hat is passed by having each Player take it off the head of the Player to his left with his left hand then put it on his head with the same hand; the volleyball is passed to the right using both hands; the ring is lifted off the neck by the Player wearing it and placed over the neck of the Player to his right; the stick is taken with a Player's left hand (when all objects are travelling to the right), passed to their right hand, then passed to the next Player's left hand; the book is pushed with the outside of the left foot and passed left.

The objects all start with one Player: the hat on her head, the ball in both hands, the ring or hoop around her neck, the stick and book on the floor at her feet. The hat is taken first by the Player to her right, then the ball, the ring or hoop, the stick, then the book are all passed as described above. The Players pass the objects around the circle three or more times.

Add: Once the groups can repeat the moves and pass the objects, they play as a competition: the first group who gets all the objects around four times and back to where they started, wins.

Note: The method of passing must stay the same! This forces the Players to concentrate on different parts of their body from the ground up, while keeping focused on their partners, the movement of the objects, and the timing of their passes, to avoid traffic jams.

+ Various props
Skills
Clarity, Collaboration, Competition, Ensemble Play, Prop Play

Properazzi

50

This is a good introduction to displaying a prop in relation to the body, creating a physical and visual link with it, and sharing the prop – and a Player's relationship to it – with the audience.

Preparation: The Players each choose a prop and gather in front of a mirror (if a large mirror isn't available, have the Players partner up, present for each other, and give feedback). They explore ways of presenting the prop to an audience, for example: gesturing to the prop with a part of the body (hand, foot, forehead, etc.) while looking from it to the audience and back again; holding the prop whilst always looking at it, or presenting it while always looking at the audience (in either variation they should *never* take their eyes off the prop or the audience). The Players explore ways of holding the prop so it is framed by the torso, the arms or legs, or different parts of the body, such as the head and arm, leg and arm, etc. They can try making the poses physically challenging, displaying the prop in eccentric ways.

The Players give the prop display a quality or attitude, a pose that expresses strength, seductiveness, intrigue, conceit, ridiculousness, pride, love, etc. They can present it as if offering it to the audience for inspection or giving it to them as a gift. They can frame it with their clothes, holding out their coat and using it as a background to the prop's display. They could hold it up against their belly or between their teeth and gesture to it with both hands. They could lie on their back, lift their legs and set it on the soles of their feet. They could present it without using their hands, have it gripped between their legs, under their chin, their arm, etc. They should try to be more inventive, dramatic, eccentric, exotic or absurd with every variation!

The Players should explore as many presents as possible – even look at what others are doing for inspiration – then choose five that they will show.

Properazzi: Three Players wait backstage with their props. They are the *Prop Models*. Three *Properazzi* kneel at the front of the stage, one left, one centre, one right (all are off the stage). The first Prop Model makes an entrance then moves to one of the Properazzi. The Model must be specific, using eye contact or body language to make it clear which Properazzo he's posing for. He strikes a pose with his prop, holds it, and Properazzo takes his picture (says 'Click'). The Properazzi stay neutral until the Model gives them his attention. It's the Model, not the Properazzi, who leads the game; the Properazzi respond only to the Model's prompting. Once a Properazzo takes a photo, the Model moves on to another Properazzo or stays with the same one. The Model shows his five poses, then makes an exit. The next Model enters immediately and poses, then exits, followed by the last Model.

+ Stage flats or curtains, various props

Skills
Clarity, Devising, Improvisation, Leading, Physical Expression, Prop Play, Solos

51

Prop Offers

This is a good exercise for developing stories using objects. Everyone feeds into the improvisation, contributing ideas and props.

Tag Team, Same Prop: Three Players stand behind a table of props set onstage off to one side. The first Player picks up a prop, moves centre-stage, and starts improvising with it for the audience (using sounds is okay, but actual words aren't allowed). The improv does not have to be clever or funny, it can simply be a movement exploration with the prop. Either of the other two Players may take the first Player's place with a new idea, or a continuation of the idea or movement introduced by the first Player, but they must do so using the same prop. A new Player can also come in if their partner is struggling or invites them to take over.

At any point, the Guide can signal for someone to enter with a new prop by clapping his hands, and the Players take turns improvising with this new prop until the Guide claps again for another new prop, or signals the end of the improv.

Tag Team, New Prop, Same Scene: Same as above, but the Player who takes over must come in with a different prop while continuing the scene introduced by the first Player. The objective is to evolve the same story or movement play.

Tag Team, New Prop, New Scene: The Player who takes over must come in with a different prop and change the scene completely.

Note: The Guide encourages the Players to explore the obvious use of the prop, as well as make it into something else – a chair could become a bull, a stick turns a Player into an aeroplane, etc.

+ Stage flats or curtains, various props on a large table
Skills
Devising, Ensemble Play, Improvisation, Leading, Prop Play, Timing, Trios

PART NINE

PHYSICALITY

Exploring and improving physical expressiveness

For actors trained in script-based theatre, words are paramount. Clowns, on the other hand, are physical, visual players. Their main means of expressing themselves is via their bodies, their facial expressions, their gestures, and the use of props and scenic elements. Clowns might use words to develop their rapport with an audience, but words are not their dominant form of communication – they're just one more way for clowns to connect.

In our day-to-day life we rarely use our bodies in an expansive way to express emotions, so we haven't built up the muscles to hold a strong pose or a facial expression that communicates powerful feelings of jealousy or joy, anger or sadness. We are 'out of shape' with regard to physical expression.

The exercises in this section are important for developing a greater emotional range and expressing that physically – and, through repetition, they'll help build the necessary muscles to do so.

Pass It Round

52

This exercise requires the Players to physicalise their emotions using their entire body, and, like Game 39: Nice and Nasty, it emphasises the importance of transition moments and connecting with the audience.

The Players stand in a circle. The Guide makes a face and assumes a strong pose using his entire body to express an emotion. He shows this to everyone in the circle (the audience), then turns and shows the face and pose to the Player to his left. She reacts physically to his emotion and its physical expression, shows her reaction to the audience, changes her pose and face *for the audience* (still facing outwards, not yet turned to the next Player), then turns and shows the new pose and face to the next person. This pattern continues around the circle.

Note: The Guide should be a stickler for the transition moments: the Players want their audience to see what is being offered before *offering it.*

Side-coaching

- Part of the enjoyment of this exercise is the moment of transition: the Players should take time to show the audience their reaction, then show them what they're going to offer to the next Player *before* they offer it. This creates an anticipation as to what will happen next and helps draw the audience in, building curiosity and suspense.

- The Players should be encouraged to go outside their physical and vocal comfort zone – and to provoke others to do the same. Be eccentric, goofy, glorious, etc.

Skills
Clarity, Devising, Duos, Improvisation, Listening, Physical Expression

Embodied Image

This exercise uses image visualisation to develop poses, movements and gestures, exploring ways to find a greater physicality using imagined objects or the natural world.

The Players are scattered about the room. The Guide asks each of them to contemplate an image: it could be an object like a large red ball, a straw broom, a broken washing machine, a rusty hammer; or something in nature like a rough sea, a huge ancient oak tree, a snow-covered mountain, a massive round boulder... The Players should be specific, contemplating not just a flower but a vigorous climbing rose, for example. They let the image fill their mind and gradually assume a pose that they feel represents the image, doing an inventory of their body as they visualise, getting *everything* involved, from their fingers to their eyes, their tongue to their toes.

From the still pose, the Players search for movements, gestures, and a way of walking. The Guide sets a length of time for each exploration, then asks the Players to let it go, take a few deep breaths and try a new image. The Players work to connect all parts of the progression: image to still pose to gesture to movement.

There may be a tendency to make fun of this kind of exercise – 'Act like a tree! Be a palm leaf!' – especially with clowns – but the Players should take it seriously and use their imaginations to trigger changes in the body and eccentric ways of moving.

Note: Imagining themselves as something in nature – something elemental – and engaging fully with the struggle of figuring out how to physicalise this, can give the Players insights on ways of moving and speaking that they may have never thought of if they were thinking only of physical play based on a human type. This can easily be developed into eccentric, comic play.

Skills
Breath Work, Devising, Improvisation, Physical Expression, Solos

54 Wind-Up, Stall, Repeat, Breathe

These are techniques for focusing the audience's attention on a moment or an action. Just as a verbal set-up prepares the audience for a joke's punchline, these techniques can be used as the set-up for physical comedy. They can also express the inner state of a clown through movement and gestures.

Wind-Up: This comes before executing an action. The movement is a reversal, the opposite of the action. For example, we inhale before speaking, we step back before running, we draw our arm back before throwing a ball. Whether obvious or subtle, short or long, a physical Wind-Up creates anticipation and suspense for the audience, preparing them for the action that is to follow and giving the action more focus.

The *Wind-Up* has a forward energy: everything is focused towards what's going to happen next.

Stall: This is a series of gestures and movements that a Player does before getting to the task at hand; tugging at their clothes, cracking their knuckles, gratuitous stretching, combing their hair, scratching themselves, etc. are some examples of stalling. Stalls do a number of things: they allow the audience to focus on what's coming, or they can distract them from it (the way magicians will use misdirection to focus attention on their left hand while they hide what their right hand is doing). Stalls can build suspense, create moments of status play, reveal the Players' thoughts and feelings, and can be developed into comic business.

The *Stall* has a distracted, deflecting quality: the Player is avoiding what's going to happen next.

Repeat: This is a single gesture or a short series of movements. They are physical habits that can express something about the Player's inner state or personality: smoothing down the hair can express a Player's vanity, or, if they're nervous, they anxiously slick down their hair again and again as they prepare to do a difficult task. Repeats can also be functional:

the Player's hair is sticking up and they want to keep it down; or the action can be a way of playing with the audience: they see someone in the crowd and feel the need to slick down their hair.

Repeats can be used as a Wind-Up: slicking down the hair before approaching a love interest; or as a Stall: slicking down the hair, the clothes, the carpet, the curtains, the dog, etc. because the Player is too nervous about approaching a love interest.

Breathe: This is making an inhalation or exhalation obvious. We hear the sound and see the body contracting (exhale) or expanding (inhale). It can be worked into an act or scene as a Wind-Up, Stall or Repeat (and as a way for a Player to remind themselves to breathe in a scene).

Any of these techniques can be used with most any exercise in this book, especially solo, duo and trio work. They can be choreographed into a scene or used as side-coaching during an exercise: the Guide can interrupt what's going on and call out, 'Wind-Up!... Stall!'

Note: George Carl is a master of the stall. Art Carney and Jerry Lewis were also brilliant at it. The Wind-Ups and Stalls of both these comedians were doubly enhanced by the reactions of their partners (Jackie Gleason and Dean Martin) who grew visibly irritated by their antics.

Using Take, Wind-Up, Stall, Repeat, Breathe: Go to Game 22: *Takes*. When you see the object, work in a Wind-Up, Stall, Repeat or Breathe. Each time you cross the stage, try a different one, or play with variations of the same technique. Use these techniques with any of the exercises that utilise tricks or tasks (see Games 44–47, and in the *Solo, Duo, Trio* and *Ensemble* sections).

+ Stage flats or curtains, various props

Skills
Breath Work, Clarity, Devising, Improvisation, minimum-to-MAXIMUM, Physical Expression, Timing

55 Pick a Mask

A good exercise for developing the facial muscles and connecting the external to the internal.

The Guide puts tables or chairs around the room. On each table or chair she lays index cards that have energies written on them that could be played as fixed faces or masks, for example: happy, angry, lusty, sad, joyful, proud, paranoid, cute, etc. (there can be multiple cards of the same mask). The Players imagine what each face would look like. After they've looked over the labels, they choose one, cupping both hands over the label as if lifting a mask. They put it on. Their face assumes the expression of the energy on the label. They lift their head and draw their hands away, revealing this mask. Once it's on, the Players shouldn't change the expression of the mask; it's a fixed face, only the eyes move. In a mirror, the Players examine the mask for a few moments – and their body in relation to it – then remove it with both hands. They place the mask on the label and choose a new one. The Players try a few, then put the same ones on again, transforming their face into the same mask. Does their face remember it?

Now the Players switch between masks a bit faster. How well can they recall each face?

Note: An important part of this exercise is learning how to keep the face fixed: the face wants to move, to react. The Players should strive to use the body, gestures and the breath to express reactions or degrees of an energy and keep the face still.

This exercise trains and strengthens the muscles in the face, and helps the Players explore the interplay between the face and the body in expressing emotions. Improving the expressive power of the face in connection with the body is crucial for clown and physical comedy.

If a Player's facial muscles get tired while doing the exercise, they shouldn't just relax the face but use their hands to remove 'the mask' first.

Side-coaching

- Once the mask is on, nothing should change on the face. The Players respond to things around them without changing their facial expression; to achieve different emotions they alter the angle of the head or the shape of the body.

- The Players should find the best moments to switch from mask to mask to express a change in emotion, or from the mask to the Player's own (mobile) face, for dramatic or comic effect.

- How is the breathing affected by the different masks? How can the Players use the breath to enhance the experience of the mask for themselves and the audience?

- Let the mask affect the inner state, then show us the inner state using the fixed face and the body.

- This exercise will help in scenes where a Player needs to express a series of strong emotions in quick succession; switching the face first can help them achieve this.

+ Tables or chairs, index cards, large mirrors

Skills
*Breath Work, Clarity, Improvisation,
Physical Expression, Solos*

56

PHYSICALITY

Physicalise a Phrase

When working silently, thoughts will still arise, words will still come barrelling towards the tongue, but 'speaking' those thoughts and words with the body will help improve a Player's ability to express themselves physically. Combining this with a strong emotion, and making it a competition for the audience's attention, pushes the physical play to another level.

Three to four Players stand upstage in a line, two metres apart, their backs to the audience. If played on the same level as the audience, mark a stage edge with a rope, creating a four-metre gap between the Players and the audience.

Each Player chooses a strong energy, for example: anger, lust, confusion, irritation, joy, greed, paranoia, etc. The Guide has phrases written on cards (see below). He shows a different card to each Player *after* they've chosen an energy. The Players repeat the phrase silently, with the energy they've chosen. They turn to the audience and physicalise the phrase and the emotion behind it. They can move forward or back, left or right, but not into another Player's area. The objective for each Player is to get everyone in the audience looking at them only. After a few minutes, the Guide cues the end of the exercise by raising his hand: the Players move upstage still trying to keep the audience's attention. When they get to where they started, they say their phrase out loud using the energy they're working with, then turn their backs to the audience. Or the Guide lets the audience guess each Player's phrase once the exercise concludes.

Suggestions for Phrases

I MISSED YOU   GET OUT   I'M A LOSER

WHAT   HELP ME   DANCE WITH ME

YOU'RE PERFECT   EAT IT   LOOK AT ME

COME ON   DO YOU LOVE ME   CRAP

YOU FOOL   LET'S DO IT   I'M LEAVING

NO   YOU LIKE IT   I'M WAITING

I KNOW   OH YEAH   GO AHEAD

SHOW ME   THINK ABOUT IT   YES

56

PHYSICALITY

Side-coaching

- 'Speak' the phrase with the body. Use postures, movement, gestures, facial expressions.
- Play with the energy and phrase in combination. For example, turn the phrase '*I want you*' into a question, and the physicality expresses a desire to *get away* from the audience.
- It's not charades – the Players aren't trying to spell out the phrase for the audience; it's about *connecting* with them through emotion, physical attitude, play, and intent.
- The Players should change tactics if someone else is getting all the focus: imitate them, get bigger, smaller, change rhythm, flail about, stand still… The Players explore as many tactics as they can to get everyone's attention, while staying with their phrase and energy.

+ Index cards, tape or rope

Skills

Competition, Devising, Improvisation, minimum-to-MAXIMUM, Physical Expression

57 Party Animals

Like the earlier exercise with images, using the study of animals to enhance physical expression can lead to some quirky, visceral and hilarious play, and unique ways to express an emotion or idea with the body.

Preparation: Each Player chooses two different animals to imitate; for example, a snake and a cow, a monkey and a turtle, a dog and a lizard, etc. They observe them live or look at videos of the animals, studying how they walk, run, move their head, clean or scratch themselves, defecate, urinate, eat, sleep, the sounds they make, etc. In the session, they find a spot in the room and on an agreed-upon signal from the Guide, the Players become their first animal; they don't interact with each other but work on inhabiting the animal on their own. The Guide makes another signal, at which point the Players release the animal, relax their bodies and go back to a neutral state. The Guide signals again and the Players become their second animal, until the Guide signals for them to come out of that animal. Finally, the Guide asks them to assume their first animal and on his signal, they transition to their second animal *with no break in between*. They repeat this quick-change a few times, cued by the Guide, then try it on their own, finding reasons to transition from one animal to another (e.g. they see the colour red, stub their toe, see themselves in a mirror...).

Party Animals: The Guide lays out a table with costume pieces and accessories (no sharp edges or complicated parts, nothing fragile). The Players choose one animal and gather accessories they think will help them represent it. The objective is not to create an exact imitation but to *suggest* the animal using the costume pieces and accessories to accent their physicality.

The Guide sets up a party scene: table, chairs, some paper cups and plates, some water in a plastic pitcher. Five Players go backstage. One Player is designated *Host*. The Players are encouraged to make sounds – human and animal – keeping words to a minimum. Gibberish is fine.

Host enters first as a human with some animal traits, and arranges the space in preparation for his guests, showing bits of his animal as he prepares (keeping it subtle). The Guide makes a knocking sound: the first guest arrives, entering as a human but with animal characteristics. Host greets her, they interact.

The Guide makes another knocking sound: the next guest arrives, entering as a human but with animal characteristics.

This sequence continues with the Guide cueing each entrance. Once all guests have arrived and are interacting, their animals start to leak out. For example, when they get excited, emotional, inebriated, hungry, etc., they become even more like their animals, until the scene is a bunch of gaily dressed, highly animated, noisy beasts.

The Guide can stop the party, scolding the animals for making too much noise or behaving badly; the Players respond by reverting back to the human or staying with the animal (the Guide's intervention is part of the improv).

The Guide signals for the scene to end. The Players improvise an exit, either as animals or reverting back to human with just traces of the animal. Host is the last to leave.

Note: To use this in clown and physical comedy, a Player could base their movements, the speed of their thoughts, their timing, their physical habits, etc., on a chicken or a sloth, a monkey or a bull. The transition from a calm state to an excited one – a minimum-to-MAXIMUM – could be enhanced by the clown becoming more animal-like.

Side-coaching

- How does the animal transform back into the human, and vice versa? What is the comic or dramatic potential of the transition from one to the other?

- How do the different portrayals – accurate, subtle, exaggerated, human-animal – feel?

57

PHYSICALITY

- Use the interactions with others to spur changes from one animal to the other, and from animal to human, and back again. Choose when to change for the greatest impact or to develop the play and the scene's progression.

+ **Stage flats or curtains, costume pieces and accessories, a strong table, chairs, paper cups and plates, water in a plastic pitcher, mop, bucket and towels for clean-up**

Skills
Devising, Ensemble Play, Improvisation, minimum-to-MAXIMUM, Physical Expression, Prop Play

PART TEN

CLOWN SOLO

Developing a solo Player's skills and generating performance material

Working solo is hard: you have no one to bounce ideas off of, stimulate play, challenge or inspire you to go beyond your usual way of working. And since clowns are always seeking to relate to their audience, to engage with them to help refine their ideas, working alone in the studio can be immensely frustrating.

But if you think working on your own in the rehearsal space is hard, wait until you step out alone in front of an audience…

Because performing solo is challenging, exercises that test and agitate Players are important. The Guide, acting as Boss Clown, engages with the Players in a provocative and playful way, pushing them out of their comfort zones and encouraging different reactions, emotions and attitudes. These interactions help build confidence, preparing the solo Player for audiences that might be at best disinterested or, at worst, antagonistic. The challenge for the solo Player is to win them over, open them up to play. These exercises motivate the Players to toy with adversity rather than be shut down by it, to find joy and play in their encounters with any audience.

The following exercises also contain techniques that can help structure an act, give it greater clarity, and find ways to develop and expand ideas to help generate performance material.

Segmented

58

This exercise breaks down an act or scene into five segments to help the Players clarify their presentation.

Preparation: The Players come up with a single trick to perform; it can be anything from a three-ball juggling flash, the splits, balancing a pole, a pirouette, doing a cartwheel, throwing something high in the air and catching it, standing on one leg on top of a stool, etc. The Players will be asked to repeat it in various ways so it must be something they've mastered, not something they're learning to do.

The Players have to imagine this trick will be performed in a large theatre, so they shouldn't choose something that is hard to see in a big space. They bring in any prop they need for the trick (though it doesn't have to involve a prop); if they have a costume, they should bring that as well.

Note: The Players might want to come in with a few tricks so they can find the one that works best for the exercise.

The Segments: These are the five segments:

- *Entrance:* The Player first appears from backstage (their entire body visible).
- *Moving into the Space:* The Player moves towards the spot on the stage where they'll present.
- *Present:* The Player does their trick.
- *Leaving the Space:* The Player moves towards the exit.
- *Exit:* The Player presents a final picture of themselves just before they exit.

This whole thing should take less than a minute. The Player should keep it specific, economical, without embellishing. The objective is to decide on and execute the *essential* actions to create an act that includes one trick.

At the end of each segment, the Player should come to a complete stop – not tense and frozen, but held, as if posing for a photo.

Add: The stop is accented with a sound. For example, at the end of each segment the Player says 'Wah!'

Add: The stop is accented with a movement. For example, at the end of each segment the Player wiggles his hips. A sound or movement acts as punctuation, as if to say 'That's the end of that moment.' Only then does the Player move to the next segment. The sound or movement can act as a place to pause and bring the audience in, let them get a good look at the Player, get to know them – especially in the Entrance and Moving into the Space – before they present their trick. It's a good way to build suspense or curiosity. These moments of punctuation can be loud, big and extended or quiet, small and short.

+ Stage flats or curtains, props and costumes

Skills

Clarity, Devising, Leading, Listening, Physical Expression, Prop Play, Solos

59

The Set-Up and the Scene

This exercise builds on the last one, and shows how to elaborate on and develop an act or scene further.

The Set-Up: Once the Players have worked the five segments in a concise, clear way, the Guide asks them to develop the first two elements – the Entrance and Moving into the Space. We'll call this the Set-Up.

The Set-Up helps ensure that the audience is focused on the trick or the main moment in a scene *before* it's played. It can build suspense as it prepares the audience for what's about to happen, for example: the Player stretches as he Moves into the Space, mimes the actions required for the trick, breathes deeply while focusing intensely on the prop, etc.

The Player's actions could also have no relation to the trick or main moment in a scene at all and build to the ridiculous, making the audience wonder 'What the heck is this person going to do!?' Or it can create an expectation that the Player then reverses: she stands on the edge of a table as if preparing to do a back flip – then just steps off backwards. The Set-Up can also show how a Player feels: her Entrance and Moving into the Space reveals that she's nervous, confident, joyful, or confused, etc. The Set-Up lets us connect with the Player before she has to give her complete focus to the difficult business of her act or a crucial moment in a scene.

In terms of clowning, the Set-Up is usually the moment when the clown is revealed. Many clowns will milk this moment to the point where it is the most memorable part of their act. For some clowns, setting up and preparing themselves may be their whole act (see George Carl).

As part of the Set-Up, the Players should carefully consider how they'll come onstage, and what that might say about them and their routine or scene. Marching straight to centre-stage says something different about a Player from one who enters and moves along the edge of the stage, near the curtain.

If they're using props, does the Player come in proudly displaying them, or have them hidden in a suitcase? Are they inside their coat, or thrown on from the wings? They can stretch and shake out their body as they prepare, show the start of a trick a few times without executing it, get distracted by someone in the audience, etc. This is also a good place to play with Game 54: *Wind-Up, Stall, Repeat, Breathe*.

Once the Players have decided on their Set-Up, they then present the five segments with the added Set-Up.

+ Stage flats or curtains, props and costumes

Skills
Clarity, Devising, Physical Expression, Prop Play, Solos

The Benign Dictator

This is an expanded version of Game 44: Task and Time. *It's an excellent way to both develop and refine an act. The clock acts as a benign dictator – there's no ego involved; it doesn't judge – it simply tells a Player how long they have to play and when to exit. It's surprising how much good improv occurs when under a time constraint.*

One-Minute Act: The Players take what they've learned from the previous exercises and create a one-minute act. The Guide emphasises the importance of timing the act: 'Edit and clarify. You will be cut off if you go over one minute.'

The first Player steps backstage; as soon as he enters, the timer starts. At the halfway point, the Guide calls out, 'Thirty seconds… fifteen… ten… five…' The Player must finish his act and be *fully off the stage* by the end of the minute.

Thirty-Second Act: Same as above, but now the Players must perform their one-minute act in thirty seconds. *They must do the entire act!* They can't cut anything out. The Guide calls the time.

Fifteen-Second Act: Same as above, but the Players must perform their entire one-minute act in fifteen seconds. Now do it in ten; here, editing is allowed. Now the snapshots are important: the short version could see a Player moving rapidly from one snapshot to the next, not freezing in the pose but hitting it like a flash going off.

The Players should consider how they can shorten each segment: leap in on the entrance instead of walking, then leap to the next place on the stage. They could jump on, do their trick and jump off. The Guide encourages them to enjoy the rushed feel of the reduced time, letting it inspire comic play.

Two-Minute Act: The Players take what they've learned from losing time – editing the act down to essentials, getting rid of extraneous movements, finding a way to flow from one moment to the next – and stretch this to two minutes. They shouldn't add more tricks, but use the extra time to expand moments, reveal more about what the clown is thinking and feeling. They should develop the Set-Up to build curiosity, tension, drama, and the comic potential of the entire presentation.

The Players should also toy with speed, movement and pace: go into slow motion, do an action then do it in reverse as if they left something out, then repeat it again with the new addition. Repeat the action in slow motion but add moments – tying a shoe, eating a sandwich, putting on a coat – as if the audience missed these moments when the act was done in real time. Freeze and hold a moment and play with the difficulty of sustaining the pose, speed everything up. Simply put, *play with time…*

Most Players will obsess over the presentation of the trick rather than using the moments before and after to let the audience in, develop the story and reveal more about the person onstage. What we want to see is the clown, not a trick-performing machine, or someone just onstage to show off. Once they've worked the previous exercises to clarify their act, the Players now spend the time showing more of themselves at play.

This is a chance to experiment with *Takes* (Game 22), *Entrances and Exits* (Game 24), *The Variation* (Game 46), *Wind-Ups, Stalls, Repeat, Breathe* (Game 54).

Note: The Benign Dictator can be used to help edit and clarify any act or scene, whether solo, duo, trio or ensemble, devised or scripted.

+ Stage flats or curtains, various props and costumes
Skills
Clarity, Devising, Improvisation, Physical Expression, Prop Play, Solos

61 Shifty Solos

This exercise adds a bit of colour, variety and spice to the acts.

Preparation: The Players scatter around the room. The Guide asks them to express various energies physically. The Players shift quickly from one to the next, as the Guide calls them out.

'Happy. Show us happy.'

'Sexy. Show us sexy.'

'Dumb. Show us dumb.'

'Confused. Show us confused.'

'Wild. Show us wild.'

'Shy. Show us shy.'

'Subtle. Show us subtle.'

'Melodramatic. Show us melodramatic.'

'Scary. Show us scary.'

'Vain. Show us vain.'

Repeat this with three or more Players onstage in a line facing out, about two metres between each of them. The Guide calls out the energies and the Players show their version of each, switching when the Guide calls out the next one. This is a good way to see how different energies manifest themselves in different people, and how they interpret each one physically.

Add: Play Game 24: *Entrances and Exits*. Three Players wait backstage, entering one at a time, express their energy as soon as they enter, showing it more clearly as they acknowledge and play with the audience, then exiting. The next Player enters with the same energy as soon as the previous Player exits. The third Player takes a turn, then the Guide calls out a new energy and they go again. Or they can continue to find variations and degrees of the same energy until the Guide calls an end to the exercise.

The Act Shift: The Players present their one-minute acts. Three Players go backstage. The Guide calls out an energy – 'Sad. Show us the sad version' – and each Player goes through their five segments – Entrance, Moving into the Space, Present, Leaving the Space, Exit – with each segment expressing sadness, for example: how would sadness affect the way a Player enters, how would they do a sad cartwheel, how would the energy affect the way they exit? As soon as they leave, the next Player enters expressing the same energy in their act. After all have gone, the Guide can call out a new energy or let another trio go.

+ Stage flats or curtains, props and costumes

Skills

Clarity, Devising, Improvisation, Physical Expression, Prop Play, Solos

Solo Variations: Atmospheres

This is a series of atmospheres or settings to apply to an act or scene to change the way it's presented. It can be used for the entire scene or just a segment, and will help generate new ideas.

With Reverence: The Players present their one-minute act or scene as if it were a holy ritual, with all the reverence, piety and magnificence of a religious ceremony. They shouldn't present it in a mocking fashion, nor use any gestures or props that reference a particular faith; instead, they must create their own reverent ritual, treating their props with high regard, creating their own significant gestures, with their act as the final offering.

The Players should work the five segments – Entrance, Moving into the Space, Present, Leaving the Space, and Exit – to establish an atmosphere of veneration. If it gets laughs that's fine, but the Players shouldn't play for laughs; they must take what they do seriously, imbue every moment and every prop with solemnity, high drama and theatricality.

Olympic Event: The Players present their one-minute act as if it were an Olympic event: they enter as if stepping into a stadium – the line of their body, the way they acknowledge the massive crowd – should all communicate the size and importance of the setting.

The act is presented with the energy of a race: the entrance is a sudden burst from backstage; the Player moves quickly into the space and presents the act or scene with the focus required of a win-or-lose, I've-been-training-for-this-moment-since-I-was-five-years-old level of intensity! It all moves at a brisk pace; the Player is trying to 'win' by putting forth the kind of effort a sporting event like a race requires (not rushed in a panicked way, but with a strong, focused, forward momentum). After the trick, the Player acknowledges the cheers of the crowd, grateful for having completed 'the race'. She tries to catch her breath, come down from the adrenaline high, as she makes her exit.

The Players should watch sporting events and take notes: what are the physical, mental and emotional preparations for the athletes? What's going on with their bodies, their faces? Take note of the athletes' actions during the competition itself. The Players should watch sports that require a sudden burst of energy – such as a hundred-metre sprint, discus throw, long jump, etc. – and copy some of the same movements and moments athletes involve themselves in, then include variations of them in the acts.

Note: These can be used to develop a way of playing any activity in a scene: walking the dog, washing dishes, brushing hair, folding bedsheets, etc.; all can be played with reverence and/or as an Olympic event. These atmospheres are useful for creating whole scenes, or as a break in the midst of a longer scene when suddenly everyone starts putting on their coats and hats whilst playing as though they are trying to win a hundred-metre dash.

Teatro Grande: The Players are asked to imagine this setting: the Teatro Grande, one of the most opulent stages in the world. There are a thousand seats in the theatre – five hundred on the main floor, three hundred in the balcony above, one hundred on a long balcony to the left and on a long balcony to the right. The house is packed! The audience have come to witness greatness…

A Player must physically present herself in such a way as to express the size and configuration of this grand theatre, and the great expectations of the audience. The Player's upper body is lifted and open, her gestures graceful and grand. Throughout the presentation, the Player acknowledges and plays to the balconies as well as to the main floor. Poise, grace and economy in movement are essential in such a space in order to be read from all parts of the theatre. The line and form of her body must be expansive, her footwork clean and grounded, her every gesture focused, extended and *filled* with energy! The Player acts with confidence without being arrogant, playful without being silly or comic, effusive without being cheesy. Her energy is similar to a confident circus artist or opera diva: immense self-love coupled with a great love for the audience.

The Players present their solo acts for this grand theatre (doing a coin trick will not read). They must play with full commitment – physical, mental and emotional. Every moment, every part of the act – costume, props, music, the space itself – holds the utmost importance. The presentation is graceful, elegant, and grand; the Players are confident and at the same time, vulnerable; there is always the possibility that things won't go as planned…

Note: Physical training in dance, acrobatics, Alexander Technique, and mime are useful in this exercise as they emphasise good alignment, poise, and the physical presence that comes from a strong core and good posture.

Side-coaching

- The Players should watch religious ceremonies to get the feel for how participants enact the ritual. They're looking for information so they can invoke a similar atmosphere in their act. They should pay attention to all details: movement, sound, objects, clothing, props.

- The Players can use music but be aware of how it affects what they do; treat it like a living partner who makes suggestions. It's best to choose music without lyrics so the audience is not distracted by what is being sung but can focus on the performance. The music should not lead or dominate the act but rather support and *enhance* it.

- The Players should find a costume that shows them off in a way appropriate to their presentation. They should spend time rehearsing in the costume so it does not cause any problems. Like the music, it's meant to enhance, not distract.

- Props can be preset or brought on; the Players should decide which is strongest for their act.
- If something goes wrong, the Players shouldn't apologise or lose their poise. They deal with the problem and continue with the act, confidently and with grace. What is crucial to note is how mistakes are acknowledged, and how the Player recovers and carries on with their presentation – they should be the ultimate professional.

+ Stage flats or curtains, various props and costumes

Skills
Clarity, Devising, Physical Expression, Prop Play, Solos, Timing

Seven Snapshots

This helps clarify an act even further and helps the Players understand the importance of stillness, strong physical attitudes and visual play.

Once the Players know their act or scene and have developed it in the Set-Up, they now break it down into a series of seven 'photos' – strong, expressive and dynamic still poses. The Guide talks them through the sequence.

- *Entrance:* This still pose says something about who you are, how you feel and how you might present your act. Or it creates an expectation that you fulfil or up-end by doing something unexpected.

- *Moving into the Space:* This still pose continues to give information about who you are, and expresses movement and energy as you come into the space.

- *The Set-Up:* This still pose creates curiosity or suspense about what you're going to do.

- *The Act:* This still pose gives a good idea of what the act is.

- *The Big Moment:* This still pose shows the high point or finale of the act, the climax of the scene.

- *Leaving the Space:* This pose expresses movement and energy as you leave the space after the Big Moment, and how you feel about what just happened.

- *The Tag Before the Exit:* This pose offers a final picture of you just before you exit, one last look at how you feel after your act.

The Players should give each snapshot an energy and make sure each pose expresses it. Here's an example:

- *Entrance:* The Player leaps onstage, lands with a thud and strikes a pose expressing anger, a pillow clutched tightly in both fists.

- *Moving into the Space:* She holds the pillow over her head, leg raised as if stomping her way to centre-stage.

- *The Set-Up:* She's glowering at the pillow.
- *The Act:* She's twisting and strangling the pillow with both hands.
- *The Big Moment:* The pillow's on the floor and the Player stands over it, foot pressed on it like a hunter who has just killed her prey!
- *Leaving the Space:* She holds a still pose of walking with her head held high, defiantly satisfied! The pillow lies flattened and torn on the floor, still onstage.
- *The Tag Before the Exit:* The Player shows one last defiant look at the pillow.

The Players should find as many physical variations as possible: stand tall, lie on the floor, squat, have the limbs stretched out in different directions, go into a lunge, curl up in a ball, lie down with the prop held high, etc. Choose different places on the stage for each photo. Consider what each pose and position says about how you feel in that moment.

Once the Players have their seven photos, have them partner up and show them to each other, taking just a few seconds between each photo to set up the next shot. Partners may offer suggestions as to how to enhance the photo by asking the Player to hold the prop differently, move to a different spot on the stage, contract or expand their body, angle themselves in a different way, have a stronger facial expression, etc. Observers should keep in mind not only the Player's body but how they use the space and the scenic elements (e.g. a chair, a stage flat). The Guide sets a time limit for each partner to show their seven photos and get feedback, then the Players show them to the group. They hold each photo until the Guide signals them to change.

Note: The Players can take actual photos of each pose to help remember them, and to allow them to look at each pose themselves and consider what works best.

CLOWN SOLO

Side-coaching

- The Players should make the snapshots full of information about how they feel, what they're doing, what they want the audience to know or what will make them curious, build suspence.

- The Players look for variety in each snapshot: change the line and level of their body, have a different expression on their face for each photo, alter their clothes – they start with the shirt tucked in, end with it wrapped around their head or stuffed into their mouth. They change location: if one photo has them centre-stage holding three juggling clubs, the next could show them at the stage-right corner, on the floor, reaching out to the audience, one club held in their teeth. The snapshots represent a series of actions that tell a story or excite the audience. The objective is to engage the audience, make them curious about the full act or scene.

+ Stage flats or curtains, various props and costumes

Skills
Breath Work, Clarity, Devising, minimum-to-MAXIMUM, Physical Expression, Prop Play, Solos

PART ELEVEN

CLOWN DUO

Developing partner relationships and generating performance material for duos

It has happened on a number of occasions with a student who is struggling: I find the right partner for them and they suddenly burst forth with ideas and joyous play!

A duo's relationship can take many forms: two fools of equal ineptitude; the clueless Boss and his clever Fool; the devious schemer and her naive partner – to name just a few. Their union can be enhanced by the joy they find in playing off one another, or by the way their antagonism is converted into feisty comedy.

Duo exercises allow the Players to explore what different partners bring out of them, and can have an enormous effect on the development of their clowns.

When choosing partners, try matching fast or anxious with slow or thoughtful, anxious with anxious, slow-witted with slow-moving, etc. Consider the visual and the physical: thin with chubby, muscular with spindly, tall with short, mean-looking with sweet-faced. Some duos can walk onstage and get a response simply because of the visual contrast or underlying harmony (or disharmony) between their look and their perceived energy.

These exercises also explore status and ways of using it to generate performance material.

64

Walk Like Me

This exercise encourages partners to get to know one another through observation and imitation; this information can be used later in a clown routine to create synchronised movement or a chorus effect, or clowns can use the information in a playful way to make fun of each other.

Observers: The Players partner up and find space in the room to work. One Player – *Walker* – walks in a natural way. The other – *Observer* – watches with these questions in mind: What part of the body does Walker lead with? For example, are their hips pushed out in front of the rest of their body, or is it their head that extends forward? Where do they hold tension? What's the shape of their spine? How do they hold their shoulders, their pelvis? How do they move their arms? What's the expression on their face? What is the tempo of their walk? Observer looks at Walker from all sides, taking in as much detail as possible. Observer shares what she sees with Walker and asks him to exaggerate it. For example, if he holds tension in the shoulders, ask him to tense up more; if he leads with the pelvis, ask him to push it out further; if he has a slow tempo, have him slow it down more; if he swings one arm more than the other, exaggerate that. Walker explores the exaggerations then returns to his normal gait; the Players then switch roles.

Imitation: Observer walks behind Walker, imitating him based on what she has seen, continuing the exploration as they walk. When Observer feels she has it, she lets Walker know: he steps out and watches. Once both the Players feel the walk is accurate, Walker follows Observer, imitating the person imitating him. Then they both exaggerate the walk; the Players then switch roles and start again.

Guesswork: The Players walk around the room. The Guide calls out a name: that Player chooses another Player to imitate, but doesn't make it obvious who it is (i.e. don't follow right behind them or stare at them). Once the Player has a strong imitation, the Guide tells the other Players to follow his imitation (this leads to the one who is being imitated imitating herself). When the group is in sync, the Players guess who is being imitated. When they get it, the Guide says 'Neutral' and everyone goes back to their own walk. The Guide calls out another name and they start a new exploration. Continue through the whole group.

Note: The Guide should make it clear to the Players that these observations are not judgements or critiques; the Players are trying to help each other to see themselves as others see them, to give feedback in an honest, constructive way. Each Player can use the information to develop greater physicality and a more expressive body.

Side-coaching

- The Players should work to be as accurate as possible in their imitation to help Walkers better understand their own physicality.

- These observations can help the Players to get to know their partners and improve their connection.

- Observers can borrow the physicality of their partners to help them get beyond their own physical habits and move in more diverse ways.

- This kind of physical work can help duos find ways of connecting by understanding each other's energy through imitation. It can also give an audience visual clues as to a duo's relationship.

+ Stage flats or curtains
Skills
Collaboration, Duos, Following, Listening, Physical Expression, Trust

Cane Connection

This is a simple exercise that helps partners get connected physically and focuses their attention on that connection.

Finger–Cane–Finger: The Players each find a partner and place a one-metre-long stick between them. They stand two metres apart, facing each other. The Guide signals the Players to start. They approach the stick, moving towards opposite ends. They place their index finger against the tip of their end of the cane at the exact same time and lift it together. They begin to move the cane, exploring ways of moving together, varying who leads and who follows, as well as playing with situations where neither partner leads nor follows. The Players explore levels – raising the stick high in the air, or going to the floor and lying down, or one Player could stand while the other lies down. They could both roll across the floor while keeping contact via the stick. The Guide encourages them to play with fast and slow, flowing and staccato, and big and small movements, etc.

If the cane is dropped, the partners take a breath together, pick the cane up, and start again. The Guide signals the end of the exercise. The Players then try again with new partners.

Other Parts: Played the same as above, but the Players place the stick against different parts of their bodies: palm-to-palm, forehead-to-forehead, belly-to-belly, etc. They should also try with each Player using different body parts: one has the point of contact on the palm of their hand, the other on their forehead, etc.

Blind: Try playing any variation with eyes closed.

> **+ One-metre long bamboo canes or other lightweight sticks with tape and a bit of padding, or rubber stoppers on each end**
>
> **Skills**
> *Collaboration, Duos, Improvisation, Introductions, Listening, Prop Play*

Mirrors and Shadows

Mirrors is a classic exercise because it is both fun and informative: you can learn a lot about a partner by following and mirroring their movements. Shadows is an exercise I developed after watching master clowns like Charlie Chaplin and Buster Keaton following – or being followed by – their bigger, heavier, antagonists. It's a simple but effective way to visually connect two Players for the audience, and can help them develop their relationship and create comic play.

Mirror Me: Partners face off. One Player is *Leader*, the other, *Mirror*. Leader begins to move. Mirror imitates *exactly* what is shown, *adding nothing*. The Players explore movement only: they don't act out a scene. The Guide reminds Mirror to pay attention to everything: facial expressions, the position of the feet, the shape of the spine, how the hands are held, etc. The Guide signals to the Players to switch roles.

Switches: In this version, the Players switch between who is Leader and who is Mirror on their own with no signal from the Guide. Instead, she encourages them to make the switches obvious (e.g. Mirror makes a sudden movement, no longer imitating Leader). They then try making the switches without any obvious cueing, until partners are not sure who is leading and who is following. Now the Players can play in two states, feeling a sense of freedom that they can move how they want (Lead), but with an awareness that they must also follow (Mirror) what their partner is doing. This is difficult at first, but it can lead to a wonderful feeling of connection.

Little Mirror: The Players imagine the mirror is small – about 30x25 centimetres – and is suspended in the air between them. This allows them to isolate just a part of the body: Leader mimes moving the mirror to her hand and Mirror reflects only Leader's hand. Or Leader moves it down low and Mirror reflects only her foot, her knee, etc., and does not worry about mirroring the rest of the body. Leader can shift the position of the mirror to make their exchange easier or harder. For example,

Leader puts it waist-high and lifts his foot up to it, while trying to keep balance, or puts it down low so both the Players have to lie on their stomachs to bring their faces towards the mirror. This is a good way to work on physical isolations, develop an awareness of a range of movements in a body part, and warm up different areas of the body.

Wandering Mirrors: The Players wander around the room. At any point, any Player can step in front of another and take on the role of Mirror and start to imitate their chosen partner. She can accept Mirror and become Leader or walk away. Mirror can keep trying to imitate the Player, or move on as well. If a Player accepts Mirror, they play the Mirror game in place for a few moments, then one or both break away and start walking, looking for a new partner. The Guide encourages the Players to explore both long sequences – 'Get to know your new partner before moving on!' – as well as short sequences – 'Mirror for five seconds then move on!'

Shadow: The Players partner up, one is *Leader* the other, *Shadow*. Leader begins to move about the room with her partner walking in sync, shadowing (mirroring) everything she does from behind her. Leader plays with stops, suspensions, takes and gestures to give her Shadow plenty to respond to. Shadow should also play with proximity: be right up close behind Leader as she walks, or be further away still shadowing every move.

Shadow has a mind of his own as well. For example, Leader may point at something and Shadow moves towards it, away from imitating Leader. But Leader was only pointing it out. She grabs him and moves him back behind her (status play). Or Leader may indicate to Shadow to pick up something by pointing at it, but Shadow just imitates the pointing. Leader gets frustrated and responds by pushing Shadow towards the object. Shadow pushes Leader back. He apologises. Or they start to tussle! It starts as an exercise in following and mirroring, and can expand into, and develop, a relationship between two Players, both in terms of physical play and status. The Guide signals to the Players to switch roles.

Note: The Players should not speak in any variation; sounds are okay but they should avoid discussing or commenting on their actions. Instead they should focus on communicating with their eyes, their bodies, and their movements.

Side-coaching

- In all variations, Leader should start slow, helping the one following them (Mirror or Shadow) by not moving too abruptly, trying to find a flow to the movements so their partner can follow. Enjoy being in sync then start to explore how to disturb that harmony without losing it completely.

- The one following should keep a keen eye on Leader and concentrate on every aspect of their body: spine, face, arms, hands, legs, feet, etc. Work to achieve a total awareness of what Leader is doing and feeling.

- Shadowing is an exercise as well as a mini-scene. The Players provoke each other by toying with the rules: Shadow is supposed to follow Leader but sometimes steps out on his own; Leader instigates everything but may also allow Shadow to go off on his own, before reminding Shadow that *he* is meant to be following *her*.

- Both the Players can deliberately set themselves up: Leader can play with a variety of movement and gesture, as well as rhythm and speed, to challenge Shadow, then get irritated when Shadow can't keep up or gets things wrong. Shadow can stop following and just watch Leader, or go off on his own, allowing himself to be reprimanded or punished for his independence. Maybe Shadow does things wrong because he's confused. Maybe he does them because he wants Leader's attention.

Skills
Collaboration, Devising, Duos, Following, Improvisation, Leading, Listening, Status

67

Dogged

This exercise uses the familiar relationship between a dog and his master to explore status play.

Doggie: The Guide sets a chair and a small, sturdy table onstage. Two Players wait backstage. The first Player to enter is *Master*. He comes in, sits down and reads his newspaper (he can also have a second newspaper rolled up and taped shut, and a paper cup half filled with water). The second player is *Dog*. She enters and wants attention, wants to play, get fed, wants water, etc. The Players explore their relationship using the various props, and play the tension between reward and punishment for different actions. They find an ending or the Guide signals them to end and exit.

Doggish: Same set-up as above. One Player is *Master*, the other is her *Servant*. Servant is human but *dog-like*: they play with subtler versions of tail wagging, panting, paws up, cowering, jumping on furniture, etc., but as a human. The Players enter one at a time or together. The scene can start simply: Servant enters and cleans up, offers the Master a newspaper, offers a chair, serves a cup of water from a tray, etc.

The Players use the discoveries from the first variation to play the scene, with Servant using some of the same tactics a dog would use without actually playing a dog: Servant wants affection, a reward for good behaviour, tries to avoid getting beaten when they do wrong. Master toys with Servant, playing the game of reward and punishment. Both the Players find ways of making the interplay overt as well as subtle. How does Servant use their low status to get what they want? How does Master keep from becoming a cruel taskmaster, acting more parental instead? The Players find an ending, or the Guide signals them to finish the scene and exit.

Side-coaching

- Find moments where Dog obeys Master: don't just play Dog as a bounding, out-of-control pet. The status relationship must have stakes: for Dog, the threat of getting beaten, not being fed, loved, etc.; for Master, Dog biting, leaping on furniture, chewing up the paper, not showing affection…

- How can Dog/Servant play low status in order to get their way (and attain a higher status over their Master)? What can Dog/Servant do to manipulate Master to get attention, love?

- When Dog/Servant gets their way or does something they aren't supposed to, how do they revert back to low status so as not to be punished? How does Dog/Servant physicalise this transition? How does Master use the threat of punishment to control Dog/Servant and assert her high status? How does Dog/Servant use these threats to achieve high status, for example, by getting the audience's sympathy?

Note: Status play is important in clown and physical comedy, and finding ways to take advantage of status in a scene – whether high or low – is crucial.

+ Stage flats or curtains, newspapers, paper cups and water, a chair, various props

Skills

Competition, Duos, Following, Improvisation, Leading, Prop Play, Status

68 The Solo Duet

This is a good exercise for getting the Players to block out an act or scene by choosing strong, dynamic poses. It's also good for seeing which Players might make good partners as it allows them to be seen side-by-side; their physicality and expressiveness can support and contrast each other in playful ways.

My Mirror: Each Player creates an act or scene: they can take a section from something they've done before, or make up something in the session, keeping it simple enough that it can be easily repeated and copied by a partner. The Players then break their act down into a series of five snapshots – strong, expressive and dynamic still poses that show the Entrance, Moving into the Space, the Present, Leaving the Space and Games Exit (see Games 58 and 60). The Players should give each snapshot an emotion and ensure the pose expresses it, for example: a pose where the Player is kissing his hat and the emotion is *love*.

The Players partner up. Each teaches their partner the act through the snapshots, working together to ensure they mirror pose, face and energy down to the last detail; the Players are encouraged to transform themselves into the other person completely! They then present the pieces to the group with the Mirror performing alongside her partner. When they've gone through the series, the second partner shows his snapshots with his partner as Mirror.

Mirror Play: Partners enter. The first Player presents his full act, with the Mirror waiting for the moments when he can join in by snapping into the poses they've worked out between them. Mirror stands in a neutral state to one side and slightly behind their partner, and when a 'snapshot moment' comes up, both the Players strike the pose and hold this for a few seconds before continuing with the act. The poses help create a more dynamic and connected play between them. The Players can work the timing of the snapshots so they *explode* out of the routine, as they both snap into the still poses, or they reveal the snapshots slowly, in a more subtle way.

They can also play it as a game, with the Mirror either making fun of her partner, or encouraging him, overenthusiastically striking the poses alongside him.

Side-coaching

- Create strong snapshots by choosing dynamic poses that make the audience curious as well as giving them information about each Player and their act.
- Remind Players to scan their partner's entire body when mirroring: how are their feet positioned, what does each part of their face express, where does their partner hold tension, where do they extend, where do they compress, etc.

+ Stage flats or curtains, various props and costumes
Skills
Clarity, Collaboration, Devising, Duos, Following, Leading, Physical Expression, Timing

PART TWELVE

CLOWN TRIO

Exploring status and the dynamics of a trio

The trio is one of the most well-known of clown partnerships. They've been given names – Whiteface, Contra Auguste and Auguste – and numbers – #1, #2, #3.

I call them *Boss*, *Negotiator* and *Fool*.

The trio gives more opportunities to explore and expand status play, with each clown jockeying for position and attention (from each other and the audience). This gives the scenes a heightened energy, the playing becomes more dynamic. Each action in the scene becomes a provocation, as the clowns toy with their status within the group, and how the audience perceives and responds to the trio and each individual clown.

When it comes to status play and relationships, the trio provides a number of variations: Boss can team up with Negotiator and abuse Fool. Fool and Boss can laugh at Negotiator's attempts to make peace. Fool and Negotiator can make fun of Boss. They can play as three solos trying to win over the audience. They can play together in harmony, all of equal status.

A third clown puts everything off-balance, forcing the Players to pay greater attention to what's going on, encouraging a deeper connection with their partners.

These exercises will help develop connections between partners, generate performance material for a trio act, or for three-person scenes within a larger play.

Lookers

69

CLOWN TRIO

This is trio play at its most basic: the Players engage with each other and with the audience using their eyes and simple physical play. It's a good way to begin trio work.

Turn Away: Three Players enter together, moving into the space and standing facing the audience, their shoulders nearly touching. They have two choices: they can either stay facing the audience, looking at them, or turn their backs to them and not look. Each member of the trio can choose what they want to do on their own, but can also look to each other to decide what's best for the group. The trio can do the whole scene in one place or move to any point on the stage: as a group, in pairs, or all playing from a different position on the stage.

The Players use this simple set-up to develop relationships amongst the trio and express characteristics about each Player. If they get laughs, great, but they shouldn't try to be funny. They explore how they'll relate to the audience and each other, with the main actions being the looking, the turning, and the not-looking. The Players can turn fast or slow, jump and turn, start to turn but decide not to, decide on their own or keep looking to each other to make a decision on what the group will do, etc. The Players explore this simple game until they decide to leave together, or the Guide signals them to exit.

Look Away: Three Players wait backstage. The Guide sets chairs anywhere onstage side-by-side, facing the audience. The Players can enter together or separately. They make their way to the chairs to sit. As they do this, they can look at each other but must never make eye contact. So, if Negotiator is looking at Boss and she turns to look at Negotiator, he must look away (at the audience, the chairs, the floor, etc.).

One rule to play with is, if a Player does look directly at someone, she must keep looking at them until they look back. So, if Fool looks at Boss as she makes her way to the chairs, and Boss never looks to Fool during the whole scene, Fool must keep their eyes on Boss the whole time! The looks then become a way of gaining control over someone, and that person losing status by being dominated by someone else's lack of attention. Or the one looking can stare at the other to express anger, fear, love, joy, etc., making the person being stared at feel uneasy. The one staring then gains higher status.

The looks can also be a game the trio play with one another, trying to catch each other looking. They can tease each other with the looks or they can enjoy being looked at. They can make a game of looking away just as the other turns to look back. Or they might play that they're bothered by their partner's attention and the turning to look takes on a scolding quality. Also play with proximity, staring at each other from afar, or getting right up close and staring.

Add: Decide on an action after the trio sits. For example, each Player must cross their legs and they can't leave until all three have done it. This leads to a lot of looking at legs as a way of reminding each other to cross them, or a look at their face, demanding that they get on with it and cross their legs.

Note: These simple actions can create status play that can be worked into most any act or scene. Clowns can also use this simplicity when a scene gets too busy, to focus themselves and the audience on their relationship.

+ Stage flats or curtains, three chairs

Skills

Collaboration, Competition, Devising, Following, Improvisation, Leading, Physical Expression, Status, Timing, Trios

70

Be Seated

This exercise allows the Players to explore status play in a simple setting with minimal structure.

The Guide sets three chairs side-by-side. Three Players go backstage. They decide who has the highest status – she is *Boss*. She has a newspaper or magazine. The Players enter and sit; Boss takes the middle chair. She begins to read. The other two sit idly, growing bored. They start to act up, for example: they try to read the newspaper over Boss's shoulder; or they decide to compete for the attention of Boss; or try to get her to feel sorry for them and give them a page to read; maybe they are both in love with Boss and try to express it, starting a fight, tagging or smacking each other (staying in their chairs with Boss between them); or they could start flirting with each other; they could mirror Boss, imitating what she's doing; or they could make fun of Boss when she isn't looking, etc.

Boss plays with different reactions: she tries to stay calm and continue reading; she might get strict, demanding they chill out; she could lose it and smack them with the newspaper until it's a shredded mess; maybe she's attracted to one of the Players, and returns their affection; or she cosies up to the one who isn't interested, making the one who is, jealous. The Players can get up and move, or change the seating arrangement; the objective is to provoke one another in inventive ways in order to develop the relationships and status play between the three Players. Sounds and gibberish are allowed but no intelligable words.

Note: To start with, the Players should keep physical contact to a minimum and let the play evolve (looking at each other and looking away as in the previous exercise could be an effective way to start). Let more physical play develop from this quieter beginning.

Side-coaching

- Consider pushing the scene from minimum-to-MAXIMUM, developing the relationship and increasing the play until it builds to an explosion of energy between the Players!
- Or let the interaction be more relaxed, quieter, using the eyes, physical attitudes, and simple play with the newspaper and chairs.
- Find a rhythm between strong, explosive, physical action, and the calm of sitting still and just playing with looks while Boss reads.

+ Stage flats or curtains, three sturdy chairs, newspapers or magazines

Skills

Competition, Devising, Following, Improvisation, Leading, minimum-to-MAXIMUM, Status, Timing, Trios

71 Three Coats, Three Hats and a Bench

In this exercise, the Players explore ways of making status clear through movement, prop use and physical interaction, and how to change status within a scene.

Single Switch: Three Players wait backstage. They decide who is Boss, Negotiator or Fool. Each puts on a coat and hat that they think best fits their status. The Guide sets three chairs onstage side-by-side, a coat rack or a table nearby.

The trio's entrance shows their hierarchy right at the top of the scene. They acknowledge the audience, go to the coat rack or table, remove their coats and hats, hang them up, and sit on the chairs. Every single action – removing the coats and hats, how and where they hang them, which chair they choose to sit on, how they move to their chair, how they sit, etc. – must clarify for the audience the status relationship. The trio sits for a few moments, facing the audience. At some point, one of the Players will switch status and do something that communicates their choice to the others, for example: Negotiator might suddenly stand up and start ordering the others around, signifying that she has chosen to be Boss. The other two Players work out between them who will be Negotiator and Fool. This is all improvised and decided without words (sounds or gibberish are okay). They get up, put their coats and hats back on – each move showing the new status relationship – finish the scene, and exit.

Repeat: As soon as the trio exits, the Player who was Boss at the time of the first entrance, becomes Fool. Negotiator becomes Boss, Fool becomes Negotiator. They play the scene again, improvise the status change and exit. They switch again, each Player moving up one step (always from the original line-up). The return to the stage should be quick, like a revolving door.

Note: Making the new status switch offstage and revealing it visually as the trio re-enter has great comic potential. Performers such as Marcel Marceau and Charlie Chaplin have used this offstage physical shift to great effect in their acts. In all forms of physical theatre, backstage or offstage are not dead spaces where the action stops, but opportunities for effective reveals, stage trickery, and a chance to enlarge the playing area by making use of areas invisible to the audience.

Side-coaching

- Learn to give and receive status messages within a scene.

- The Players must stay attentive to the moment that status is transferred. This is when the relationships between each Player in the trio get interesting.

- Consider how any single action could reveal status.

- Keeping the scene simple allows the Players to focus on their relationship and the play of status. They shouldn't force ideas or make it a scene right away. Let it develop out of the actions related to status: they will give the trio ideas about how to expand the scene.

- Play with making the status obvious. Play with making it more subtle. Play both in one scene.

+ Stage flats or curtains, three coats, three hats, a coat rack or table, three chairs

Skills
Clarity, Following, Improvisation, Leading, Physical Expression, Prop Play, Status, Trios

Props, People, Status

72

This exercise explores ways of establishing a prop's status in relation to other props and other Players.

Preparation: The Players form trios and decide on their status – Boss, Negotiator, Fool (this will change so don't labour over the 'right' choice). Each Player chooses a prop that might help them show their status. Working in different areas of the room, trios create tableaux with their props, considering how to give each prop the status according to that chosen by each Player. They can hold their props or stand next to them (if it's something large like a chair or table).

The prop's status won't always be obvious. For example, if Players choose a table, a chair and a coffee cup, you could say that the table has the highest status because of its size, the cup has the lowest because it's smaller and easily broken. But if you stack the chair on the table and the cup on top of that, one could say the cup has high status, visually.

Or take a hammer (Boss), nail (Negotiator), and a wood block (Fool). The hammer pounds the nail into the helpless wood. But one could use the wood block to pound the nail into the hammer's handle, or scratch a name on the block with the nail. There is no single 'right' tableau regarding a prop's status: the Players explore different arrangements, then choose three.

Player, Prop and Status: The first trio shows one tableau with their props that expresses their status in the trio; for example, Boss stands on top of her table, Negotiator sits on his chair, Fool sits under the table cradling a coffee cup.

Change, Stay: The Players take on a new status, expressing the change of status by how they change their physicality. For example, Fool stands up straight and holds his coffee cup out, Negotiator bends over and looks nervously inside it, Boss cowers on the table because they have nothing to fill it with. The Guide signals them to try more status shifts.

Change, Move: The Players choose a new status by changing their physicality *and* position. For example, Fool climbs up on the table with his coffee cup held high ready to strike, Negotiator cowers underneath the table, Boss climbs off the table and grabs the chair to defend herself.

Side-coaching

- How does the placement of the props give them status *visually*? Is it height, proximity (to audience), their position in relation to the other props? How well a prop is lit? How obvious is the status? Do we see right away that one object has higher status than the others, or is it more subtle, taking longer to determine? Is it purely subjective?

- How does the prop's placement draw our attention – is it eccentric? Or does it seem to be physically stronger, of greater value? What determines a prop's strength and value? Size, the materials, its colour, shape or the setting? What about our associations with it? Do we consider a violin higher status than a kazoo? Could that be up-ended?

- One insight to be gained from this exercise is the importance of creating strong visuals. A simple tableau of the Players and their props can say a lot to an audience even before they do anything. Imagine the curtain opening on a trio in a strong tableau with their props: information can be gained about the Players just by observing. It can give the audience a chance to get to know the trio and their world before it gets complicated with actions, sounds, words or story.

+ Stage flats or curtains, various props
Skills
Clarity, Competition, Devising, Prop Play, Status, Trios

Let Me Handle This

73

CLOWN TRIO

This exercise not only gets the Players to explore status, it asks them to find the comic play in being so overconfident that they become ridiculous.

This exercise involves four Players, a trio and one acting as the *Set-Up*. This person decides on a simple problem; for example, they have trouble sitting on a chair, can't put on their jacket, their pants, they want to stand on a table but can't get up on it, etc. They enter and within a few moments show the problem. They get frustrated or angry and cry for help. Enter *SuperSolver*. She comes in with lots of posturing, proclaiming, 'LET ME HANDLE THIS!' She attempts to help Set-Up by showing them the *one and only* way to do what they want to do, successfully. Instead she makes the problem worse. For example, she roughs them up as she tries to help them sit or gets completely tangled in their coat as she tries to show Set-Up how to put it on 'the right way'.

In the process she loses the high status she entered with and drops to a lower status. SuperSolver calls out for another SuperSolver, saying 'I know who can help!' He enters even more flamboyantly, full of confidence, saying 'You called!?' But he proceeds to make matters even worse. He calls on yet another SuperSolver who finally solves the problem. Or they all make such a mess of it, Set-Up solves it on their own. The Players end the scene and exit.

Note: This scene can be improvised or you can let the Players explore ideas on their own in groups of four, then present a rough sketch for the group, continuing to find material through improvisation.

Side-coaching

- SuperSolver is extremely confident from the moment they enter until they make the problem worse and reveal their ineptitude. This will create a strong contrast as they drop in status.
- Pay close attention to the disintegration of status as SuperSolver fails: how do they react to

the revelation that they, the great SuperSolver, cannot solve this and must cry for help? Show us how a SuperSolver feels about losing their super status: they could have a breakdown, claim they can handle it but need a little assistance, or deny they're screwing up and simply want a second opinion. How does Set-Up react to all these overconfident people making a mess of things?

+ Stage flats or curtains, various props and costumes

Skills
Devising, Ensemble Play, Improvisation, Leading, minimum-to-MAXIMUM, Status, Trios

Disadvantaged

This exercise came out of my own experiences dealing with props and how they never seemed to do what I wanted them to do. In the beginning it was extremely frustrating, but I soon began to see how the 'problems and accidents' actually led me to some very funny material. This exercise has become one of the best ways I know to find comic and dramatic tension in a scene and develop slapstick comedy.

Preparation: The Guide creates an obstacle for each Player: the objective is to hinder the Players' movement or perception in some way using objects or articles of clothing. Here are some examples:

One Player wears a blindfold or paper bag over his head, or a paper plate with a face drawn on it (but no eyeholes cut into it), held on the head with an elastic strap.

Another Player puts on a bulky, oversized coat with sleeves that extend a half-metre beyond his hands.

Wearing a long-sleeved coat, a third Player lifts both arms to shoulder-height. A stick is stuffed through both sleeves so she can't bend her arms: the Guide ties or tapes the end of the sleeves closed so the stick stays in place. Choose a stick that won't break, such as a strong broom handle or a flexible PVC pipe, and pad the ends to protect the Player's wrists.

Another Player could have tennis balls or balloons stuffed into their shirt or trousers. They may fall out (or pop) during the exercise, so make a rule that the Player must keep the tennis balls or balloons inside their clothing (they pick up any that fall out and stuff them back inside their clothes).

Or a Player puts on clothing that's too tight, or too big and loose.

A Player could also wear scuba flippers, oven mitts, carry a nearly full cup of water in one hand, etc. as they play the scene.

Notes about the space: Don't play on a high stage. Also, point out anything in the space where the Players may stub their toes, trip over or run into. The Players should be challenged but not feel in danger, and encouraged to play boldly whilst staying aware of the challenges posed by the space.

Notes on the obstacles: The objective here is to play the scene not the problem. The Players should toy with the obstacles and not get so frustrated by them that they stop playing. They should explore inventive ways of transforming the problem, not just clash with it to the point where the scene becomes only about their struggle with the disadvantage. For example, the stick in the sleeves can be turned into an eccentric way of moving or drinking tea. The tennis balls dropping out of a Player's shirt may appear to be a problem, but in the context of this exercise, the more they drop, the more opportunities for mishap and comic play. The Players thus learn to see opportunities rather than problems.

Notes on the rules: In the scene below with the coat and hat, the Player with a stick through his sleeves may drop his hat and not be able to pick it up easily. He may try to leave without it or kick it offstage. The Guide tells them they cannot leave unless they're wearing a hat. In the Party, all Guests must be served a drink and clink their cups together before drinking. The Guide shouldn't let the Players take short cuts. Enter into the problem and enjoy the struggle!

My Coat and Hat, Please: This exercise is for three Players. The Guide decides on a scene to create a mood, for example: they're going to a party, or a funeral, to work, or a wedding, etc. The Players are entering in order to put on their coats and hats and go out. They step backstage, put on their obstacles (another Player can assist them if necessary), while the Guide sets a table or coat rack with three coats and three hats. The Guide can add some unexpected items such as a scarf, gloves, a bra, etc.

When all are ready, the Players enter together, their actions and energy reflecting where they're going (party or funeral, work or wedding). They make their way to the coats and hats, and begin to put them on. They step downstage to check themselves in a large (imaginary) mirror, all using the same mirror, returning to the same place to look. When all three have on their coats and hats (and other items if Guide adds them), they do one last check in the mirror and exit.

The Party: This exercise is for four players, with one chosen as Host. Three Players (the *Guests*) step backstage right; one – *Host* – steps offstage left. They put on their obstacles while the Guide sets a table and four chairs, four paper cups, and a pitcher of water (play with the amount – just be aware of how much may have to be mopped up). The Guide can place things in a 'normal' way – chairs around the table, cups and pitcher laid out on it – or in an unconventional way – chairs stacked on top of the table, cups placed so they might fall off the table when Host reaches for them, etc. When all are ready, Host enters first.

Host prepares the space, arranging the table, chairs and cups, readying the space for her guests. The Guide makes a knocking sound to cue first Guest. He waits until Host comes to the door (the entrance from the wing). Host invites him in, and the party begins. Guide makes knocking sound, another Guest! Host goes to the door to let him in. Knocking cues continue until all Guests have arrived. Host gets them seated, gives them each a cup, and pours water from the pitcher into their cups. They play the scene – a lovely party on a lovely day – eventually finding an ending (or the Guide cues them to find an ending). The Players exit stage-right, with Host leaving last, stage-left.

In this scene, imagine if Host is the person with the stick through their sleeves: how will they serve tea or set the chairs? Do they wait for Guests to arrive and ask for help? How does the one with the bag on her head drink tea? How does she even find it on the table when she can't see it?

This exercise is an opportunity to explore different tactics and strategies for dealing with a disadvantage, and discovering possibilities for individual and ensemble comic play.

Side-coaching

- The fact that a Player can't bend their arms, or that their trousers are full of tennis balls, is just a part of who they are and how they were made. They don't draw unnecessary attention to it; it will attract enough attention without their help. They face life with this obstacle and survive, invent, thrive, play.

- The Players don't need to exaggerate or try to 'clown' the scene. Just play it as it is, with high energy. The obstacles and props will cause all sorts of problems – the Players should expand on them, embrace and revel in the struggle! Treat the disadvantages as challenges which will lead to greater ensemble play.

- These are obvious, physical disadvantages. Can you find the same level of mishap and comedy with a mental or emotional obstacle? A clown or character's fear, joy, pride, anger, frustration, etc., can impede them, creating similar levels of problematic play. By playing the scene, not the problem, the audience finds pleasure in watching the Players try to overcome a difficulty through exploratory play.

- As the Players watch others, what are the tactics they use to turn a problem into play? They can use some of the same tactics and expand on them when they step onstage.

- Taking a disadvantage and turning it into an advantage, by cleverness, accident or luck, is one of the essential survival and performance skills of a clown.

> **+ Stage flats or curtains, various props, *Coat and Hat*: Three coats and hats with a table or rack to hang them on, miscellaneous accessories such as a scarf, gloves, a handbag, etc. *The Party*: table and four chairs, paper cups, a pitcher filled with 1-2 cups of water, plastic tablecloth, mop and towels for clean-up**
>
> **Skills**
> *Devising, Ensemble Play, Improvisation, Prop Play, Trios, Trust*

PART THIRTEEN

CLOWN ENSEMBLE

*Developing complicity, group improv,
and ensemble storytelling skills*

There is great pleasure derived from watching a group of clowns, in part because they seem like such an eccentric, mismatched group of individuals, yet somehow play together. We might feel affection for them because of their obvious affection for each other, the ease in which they accept and play off one another. We may be fascinated by the odd juxtapositions of energy and emotion and the physical differences between individuals. We wonder and laugh at the amount of absurdity and invention they produce. And then there are the endless possibilities for physical – even acrobatic – play that a large group is capable of.

There is courage in numbers. There is also more potential for disagreement, argument, conflict. Factions may form – solos, duos and trios wanting their moment to shine outside the larger group. Any tension this creates should be brought out in the open, explored, and hopefully transformed into comic interaction. A clown's play is not all nice, whimsical or sweet. It should include conflict, quarrelling, healthy sparring. If these 'negative' aspects of relationships are reimagined and played with, they can lead to greater drama and depth in a clown ensemble's performance.

These exercises can help groups generate material, explore how individuals influence the group, how the Players can work as a chorus but also support duo or trio moments, as well as promote the acceptance of accident and absurdity in ensemble play.

75

Tableaux

Tableaux are extremely helpful in teaching the Players how to tell stories visually and physically. They also reveal the power of stillness and how this can be used in any scene to draw the audience in and connect them to the story and the people in it.

Types: Five or more Players get up in front of the group. The Guide calls out a type – doctors, fitness instructors, zookeepers, teachers, bankers, circus artists, sideshow freaks, thieves, rich people, etc. She claps and the group forms a tableau of these types. They form it quickly without discussion, gathering information about how to pose as a group through observing their partners. The Guide gives them a time limit and counts down. The tableau is completed and all the Players are still by the end of the count. They hold for the audience to take it in then the Guide signals for them to drop it. The Guide calls out another type, or lets a new group have a go.

Guess the Scene: The Players choose types or a scene – a fairy tale, a moment in history, a scene from a film, a nursery rhyme, etc. – and are given time to create a tableau in a short rehearsal. Each tableau is shown to the whole group, who try to guess what or who the scene represents. The Players hold their poses until the scene is guessed. If the audience cannot guess, the Players in tableau may make movements related to the scene in order to provide hints.

The Guide can have scenes written on strips of paper that the groups choose out of a hat.

Tableau Progression: This exercise is for four or more Players. The group gathers backstage, all on either the left or right side. The first Player enters and, standing close to the stage wing, he poses, illustrating an action, for example: he points and makes an angry face. As he holds the pose, the second Player enters, steps in front of him, and assumes a position that develops or complements what the first Player is doing and begins to create a scene, for example: she puts her hands out and feigns innocence, as if to say, *I didn't do it*. The third Player enters, goes to the end of the line and creates a still pose that develops the scene further. The fourth Player then does the same. Continue this with more Players or have the first Player drop his pose and move to the end of the line to add another pose. This pattern continues until all the Players have crossed the stage creating a final tableau close to the exit.

Side-coaching

- Focus not only on creating a short scene but making it visually and physically strong: find still poses that evoke dynamic action and give information. The Players should pay attention to how their individual pose relates to – and enhances – the scene the group is creating.

- The Players should consider how they lead the audience's eye around the tableau by how they angle their bodies and limbs in relation to others: fingers pointing, bodies leaning in, eyes focused on another Player, arms extended towards the group picture rather than away from it, etc.

- The Players should use their bodies *as a group* to form shapes and levels: think of triangles, with one person up high and others down low; create a circle of heads; have all bodies at right angles to each other; lift a Player and hold them aloft, etc.

+ Stage flats or curtains

Skills
Collaboration, Devising, Ensemble Play, Improvisation, Physical Expression

Machines and Slow-Motion Scenes

76

This exercise takes tableaux further into the invention and exploration of ensemble movement. It can also be used as a way to begin a scene, or to create changes in the action in the middle of a scene.

Machines: Five or more Players get up in front of the group. The Guide calls out a machine or mechanical object, for example: a car, a washing machine, a hose and sprinkler, a grandfather clock, a spaceship, a tank, etc. The Guide claps. The group forms the machine quickly (all must be part of it – no observers). No discussion is allowed. The Guide gives them a time limit and counts down. The Players must create the final shape by the end of the count.

Slow-Motion Scene: Five or more Players get up in front of the group. The Guide calls out a location, for example: a newspaper office, an Italian restaurant, a sleazy bar, a football game, a rock concert, a ballet class, a funeral, etc. The Guide claps. The group shows the location and the activity that goes on in it, in slow motion. The Players work to clarify what they're doing individually so the audience can clearly see their role, and each Player uses their actions to develop moments for the group's scene. The Guide claps to end it.

Add: The Guide lets groups rehearse machines or slow-motion scenes first, before presenting to the whole group.

Note: Creating machines or working in slow motion as a group not only improves ensemble play, it creates strong stage pictures. In terms of clowning, it can express relationships between the Players physically and visually, and lead to fun ways into or out of a scene, or it can be presented as a sudden, absurd break.

Side-coaching

- The Players should explore physical size: stand tall, puff themselves up, arms and legs wide; or they can contract, squat down, lie on the floor, etc.
- They should vary the size of the movements: move in large flowing ways, or with small, barely perceptible movements. Also try a mix: some Players moving in small, slow ways, others large and flowing, some standing tall, others contracting.

+ Stage flats or curtains

Skills

Clarity, Collaboration, Devising, Ensemble Play, Improvisation, Physical Expression

77

CLOWN ENSEMBLE

Repel and Lookout

This is a good way to create ensemble movement en masse: shapes are created as the group moves as one (like birds' murmurations), with individuals popping up out of the mass, duos or trios stepping out together, etc. It can help fill a large space with group play and movement, and could be the lead-in to almost any group scene, or simply as a way to bring individuals together quickly, with a common focus.

Solo Repel: The Players stand tightly huddled together. The Guide calls out the name of someone in the group. That person screams and runs away from the group to any point in the room, putting distance between herself and the others; she is repelled by them. The group lets the pain of separation build: they've lost a vital part of the ensemble! They call out her name, entreating her to come back, but she resists. Slowly they move towards her. She responds – she wants to escape! – but she can't move from the spot where she stopped (though she may writhe, squirm, jump up and down, etc.). Eventually the group breaks into a run and surrounds the Player, embracing her as one. Initially she resists but soon gives over to the embrace, to the joy of being part of the ensemble again. The Guide calls out the name of another Player, who screams and runs away, and the game continues until all have had a go at running away from the group.

Group Repel: The Players stand tightly huddled together. The Guide calls out the name of someone in the group. The rest of the group scream his name and run away from him to any point in the room. They make a group decision to regather and huddle at a distance from the Player whose name was called – they are repelled by him. The repelled Player lets the moment of separation build: he doesn't understand why they're repelled by him and feels a sense of loss. But the attraction is strong: he moves towards them, the group huddles closer together (they cannot move from where they've regathered), they crouch down, cry out his name, tell him to go away! The repelled Player toys with their reactions and the power he has over them. Eventually, the repelled Player breaks into a run and burrows into the group to rejoin them. They resist at first, squirming, trying to oust him, but then they give over, embracing him, happy to have him back; the group is whole again. The Guide shouts out another name, the group runs away, and the game continues until all have had a go.

Lookout: The Players clump together as a pack and move around the room at a brisk pace, always looking around them; they're curious as well as afraid. At some point, they stop as a group and crouch down. One or more Players stand up tall and look around, and then squat down again. Various Players continue this popping up and down for a few moments, then they all stand up and move around the room as before. They stop again as a group, all crouch, and one or more Players stand up tall and look around.

This is a great way to enter a space, especially if it's large or outdoors: the group moving together creates a strong visual, and the constant popping up and down gives the entrance a playful quality. This could evolve into the group coming downstage en masse, one Player (or a duo or trio) stepping out and doing something for the audience – a simple trick or just saying hello – with the group acting as a chorus, encouraging the one(s) who steps out, or afraid for them, confused by their actions, or supporting what they do and applauding them.

Skills
Collaboration, Ensemble Play, Improvisation

The Journey

In this exercise, the Players go on a journey, improvising with their partners, and their props.

Five Players each choose a prop. They lay them out across the stage, the first prop close to the entrance, the last prop close to the exit. The Players step backstage and decide what kind of journey they're going on and what the setting is, for example: a trek through a dense forest or a dangerous jungle; a hurried walk through a series of dark alleys; a stroll through alpine fields; a journey across the desert; going hunting in woodlands, etc. While they are backstage, the Guide lays a new prop amongst the others.

The Players enter clumped together and establish the setting by how they move towards the props. Sounds or gibberish are allowed, but no intelligible words. Each prop the Players come to must be used to develop the story of the journey (when the group comes to a prop, the Player who chose it decides what it is in the story).

The prop can be used for what it is, or transformed into something completely different: a stuffed toy could be a source of comfort through the scary forest, or it might be a dangerous beast; a water bottle could be a lantern to light the way or a horn to call for help. Once a prop decision is made, the Players go with it – they do not keep changing the prop to something else.

At some point in the journey, the Players will discover the prop laid out by the Guide. *This prop must be discovered by the entire group, all picking it up at the same time.* The group decides what it is and how to use it, the decision happening in the moment. When they get to the last prop, they find a finish for the scene and exit.

Note: Once they pick up the props, the Players carry each prop with them and continue to build the story as they accumulate objects. It does not mean that each prop carried forward must be involved in each scene. It is there as a possibility, brought in again when a Player sees an opportunity to use it in the next scene, provoked by the next prop on the journey.

Side-coaching

- The Players can use a prop in ways that are expected (e.g. a chair is for sitting), or transform them into something unexpected (e.g. a chair becomes the head of a monstrous beast).

- The Players shouldn't decide beforehand what the prop will be. Deciding in the moment, in front of (and with) the audience, allows the Players to enjoy the nervy thrill of discovering the prop and its use in the moment.

- The Players should clarify what each prop is by how they handle it. They don't bail out and suddenly change it: if they decide a bucket is a soldier's helmet, they stay with that throughout the scene and build on the idea as the journey continues, rather than switching it to something else.

+ Stage flats or curtains, various props

Skills

Collaboration, Devising, Ensemble Play, Following, Improvisation, Leading, Prop Play

79 The Preposterous Players

CLOWN ENSEMBLE

The scenes in this exercise are deliberately absurd to encourage the Players to dive in and enjoy being preposterous, while at the same time playing the scenes with the utmost seriousness. They're encouraged to go with impulses, both individually and as a group, being as imaginative as possible.

Five to seven Players go backstage; the Guide cues the applause and the group enters to a rapturous welcome. The Guide says 'Hello! We all admire your great skill as actors, thespians, so chameleon-like you can portray anything!' The actors all nod, full of confidence that they can indeed portray anything. The Guide says he has a short scene he would like them to perform. It has three parts. The Guide calls out the first part; the Players turn upstage, take a deep breath together, turn to the audience and begin.

There's no discussion amongst the Players about what they'll do. They simply turn and start acting out the scene, each Player going with the first thing that comes into their heads and working to align their improv with that of their partners.

Below are some scene suggestions; the Guide gives them the first part, lets them play for a bit then cues applause – the Players stop and take a bow. The Guide explains the second part, lets them play then cues applause – again, the Players stop and take a bow, quite pleased with themselves, congratulating each other. The Guide then explains the third part, lets the Players tie the three scenes together in progression, then cues applause – the actors bow and make their exit.

Note: Sounds, animal noises and gibberish are allowed, but no intelligible words.

Scene Suggestions

- Play a group of chickens / Frightened chickens / Chickens discovering a broken egg weeping over the death of the unborn chick as they clean it up.

- Washing machines / Pregnant washing machines / Pregnant washing machines giving birth.
- A pack of ravenous dogs / A pack of ravenous dogs who run into a pond, discover it's full of honey not water / A pack of ravenous dogs who run into a pond, discover it's full of honey not water, frantically lick up all the honey to keep from drowning, and crawl out of the pond, working as a pack to save themselves.
- Flies / Flies who discover a big pile of horse poop / Flies who discover a big pile of horse poop and work together to carry the whole pile to another place in the room.
- Balloons / Balloons farting / Balloons farting to the point where they totally deflate and die.
- Gorillas / Gorillas all playing on a wide piano / Gorillas all playing on a wide piano while singing an aria from *Carmen*.
- Roosters / Roosters strutting and warming up their voices as they get ready to cock-a-doodle-do / Roosters cock-a-doodle-doing to the tune of 'Twinkle, Twinkle Little Star'.

Side-coaching

- Get physical! Be preposterous! When the applause happens, return to the serious actors renowned for their greatness as they acknowledge the crowd.
- Improvise on what other Players offer; play off the audience's response. The objective is to keep the exploration alive, working together to find group moments as well as solo flights of the imagination, to enthral and win the love of the audience through absurd, outlandish play.

+ Stage flats or curtains

Skills
Collaboration, Devising, Ensemble Play, Improvisation

The Escalating Party

80

CLOWN ENSEMBLE

In this exercise, the Players explore shifts in energy and emotion as a group, building from minimum-to-MAXIMUM, and exploring how that affects the play and the scene.

The Guide sets up a table (strong enough to be stood on by at least two Players), paper cups, a plastic pitcher with some water in it, a couch, pillows, chairs and any other scenic elements to create a living room/party scene. Five to seven Players go backstage. Each chooses an emotion they want to play, but they don't tell their partners what it will be. The Guide names one Player as *Host*.

Host enters and prepares the scene (arranging chairs, setting the table, etc.) in a matter-of-fact way, betraying no emotion. The Guide makes a knocking sound and the first Guest enters in a highly charged emotional state. As soon as Host understands the emotion, he 'catches' it, and interacts with Guest in this same emotional state, as he offers them a chair, a cup, pours them a drink, etc. The Guide makes a knocking sound and the next Guest enters with a different emotion: Host and first Guest 'catch' it, transition to it (abruptly or gradually) and play the scene. More Guests enter (each following the knocking cue from the Guide). Each new Guest causes a different emotion to percolate through the party (the Players continue to interact with each other until they notice a change in the emotion, and then all adopt that emotion).

The Players should not always look to the new Guest's entrance in order to know the new state: sometimes they let the emotion 'travel' to them as they observe how the *group* changes. Once all have entered, they act out a party scene, playing with various ways to express, expand and escalate the last emotion introduced. The Guide chooses when to cue them to end the scene. The Guests begin to leave, the group still playing the last emotion as they exit. Host is the last one to go; he can carry on with the emotion brought in by the last Guest, switch to any of the ones offered, or go back to neutral, then exit.

Note: Introducing a strong energy or emotion upon entering is useful for any scene, as it not only draws attention to the Player entering, but immediately changes the dynamic of a scene. This can make an entrance more effective in terms of the pace and the rhythm of a scene and the story it's trying to tell.

Side-coaching

- Find variations within any one emotion and different ways to express them physically to see what they provoke in other Players.
- Consider ways to use the props, furniture, the walls, the floor and any costume elements to help express the emotions.

+ **Stage flats or curtains, various props to create a party scene such as chairs, a table, paper cups and plates, a jug with a cupful of water, towels and mop for cleaning up the water**

Skills

Clarity, Collaboration, Devising, Ensemble Play, Following, Improvisation, minimum-to-MAXIMUM, Physical Expression, Prop Play, Timing

INDEX OF GAMES

SKILLS

NUMBERS REFER TO GAMES NOT PAGES

Breath Work
7. Awareness
8. Breath and Movement
10. Ha-Ha-Ha! Wah-Wah-Wah…
14. Clap It Round
21. Point of Focus
35. Snake Pit
48. Object Leads
53. Embodied Image
54. Wind-Up, Stall, Repeat, Breathe
55. Pick a Mask
63. Seven Snapshots

Clarity
13. Mouse, Cat, Dog, Horse, Eagle
19. Buf Da
20. Wide-Eyed
21. Point of Focus
22. Takes
24. Entrances and Exits
25. The Audience: Hands
35. Snake Pit
36. Orkestra
39. Nice and Nasty
45. The Eyes Have It: The Trick
49. Props-Go-Round
50. Properazzi
52. Pass it Round
54. Wind-Up, Stall, Repeat, Breathe
55. Pick a Mask
58. Segmented
59. The Set-Up and the Scene
60. The Benign Dictator
61. Shifty Solos
62. Solo Variations: Atmosphere
63. Seven Snapshots
68. The Solo Duet
71. Three Coats, Three Hats and a Bench
72. Props, People, Status
76. Machines and Slow-Motion Scenes
80. The Escalating Party

Collaboration
2. Aura
3. Hands to Hands
4. Lean On Me
5. Human Springs
6. Knot, Spiral, Pulse
7. Awareness
8. Breath and Movement
9. Count Up, Count Down
10. Ha-Ha-Ha! Wah-Wah-Wah…
12. Alien, Cow, Lion
14. Clap It Round
18. Game On
19. Buf Da
25. The Audience: Hands
28. Fox and Squirrel
29. Dragon's Jewels
30. Snatch Tail
31. Snatch the Prize
32. Pressure Points
33. Dance and Get Off the Floor
34. Body Hide
36. Orkestra
37. Who Started It?
39. Nice and Nasty
41. In and Out – But Only Two
42. Pop Goes the Beastie
44. Task and Time
45. The Eyes Have It: The Trick
48. Object Leads
49. Props-Go-Round
64. Walk Like Me
65. Cane Connection
66. Mirrors and Shadows
68. The Solo Duet
69. Lookers
75. Tableaux
76. Machines and Slow-Motion Scenes
77. Repel and Lookout
78. The Journey
79. The Preposterous Players
80. The Escalating Party

Competition
15. Chase and Tag
27. Ha-goo
28. Fox and Squirrel
29. Dragon's Jewels
30. Snatch Tail
31. Snatch the Prize
33. Dance and Get Off the Floor
34. Body Hide
35. Snake Pit
37. Who Started It?
38. The Audience: Yay! Boo!
41. In and Out – But Only Two
42. Pop Goes the Beastie
43. The Invaders
49. Props-Go-Round
56. Physicalise a Phrase
67. Dogged
69. Lookers
70. Be Seated
72. Props, People, Status

Devising
22. Takes
24. Entrances and Exits

26. The Eyes Have It: Choices
36. Orkestra
39. Nice and Nasty
40. The Provocateur
41. In and Out – But Only Two
43. The Invaders
44. Task and Time
46. The Variation
47. Incoming!
50. Properazzi
51. Prop Offers
52. Pass it Round
53. Embodied Image
54. Wind-Up, Stall, Repeat, Breathe
56. Physicalise a Phrase
57. Party Animals
58. Segmented
59. The Set-Up and the Scene
60. The Benign Dictator
61. Shifty Solos
62. Solo Variations: Atmosphere
63. Seven Snapshots
66. Mirrors and Shadows
68. The Solo Duet
69. Lookers
70. Be Seated
72. Props, People, Status
73. Let Me Handle This
74. Disadvantaged
75. Tableaux
76. Machines and Slow-Motion Scenes
78. The Journey
79. The Preposterous Players
80. The Escalating Party

Duos
2. Aura
3. Hands to Hands
4. Lean On Me
5. Human Springs
30. Snatch Tail
31. Snatch the Prize
35. Snake Pit
39. Nice and Nasty
43. The Invaders
44. Task and Time
47. Incoming!
52. Pass it Round
64. Walk Like Me
65. Cane Connection
66. Mirrors and Shadows
67. Dogged
68. The Solo Duet

Ensemble Play
6. Knot, Spiral, Pulse
7. Awareness
8. Breath and Movement
9. Count Up, Count Down
10. Ha-Ha-Ha! Wah-Wah-Wah…
11. Let's Dance

12. Alien, Cow, Lion
13. Mouse, Cat, Dog, Horse, Eagle
15. Chase and Tag
16. Eyes Closed
17. You–Me
18. Game On
19. Buf Da
23. Chain Reaction
27. Ha-goo
28. Fox and Squirrel
29. Dragon's Jewels
30. Snatch Tail
32. Pressure Points
34. Body Hide
35. Snake Pit
36. Orkestra
37. Who Started It?
41. In and Out – But Only Two
42. Pop Goes the Beastie
48. Object Leads
49. Props-Go-Round
51. Prop Offers
57. Party Animals
73. Let Me Handle This
74. Disadvantaged
75. Tableaux
76. Machines and Slow-Motion Scenes
77. Repel and Lookout
78. The Journey
79. The Preposterous Players
80. The Escalating Party

Following
3. Hands to Hands
6. Knot, Spiral, Pulse
9. Count Up, Count Down
10. Ha-Ha-Ha! Wah-Wah-Wah…
11. Let's Dance
17. You–Me
18. Game On
19. Buf Da
23. Chain Reaction
25. The Audience: Hands
32. Pressure Points
36. Orkestra
37. Who Started It?
40. The Provocateur
43. The Invaders
47. Incoming!
64. Walk Like Me
66. Mirrors and Shadows
67. Dogged
68. The Solo Duet
69. Lookers
70. Be Seated
71. Three Coats, Three Hats and a Bench
78. The Journey
80. The Escalating Party

Improvisation
- 18. Game On
- 20. Wide-Eyed
- 22. Takes
- 24. Entrances and Exits
- 25. The Audience: Hands
- 27. Ha-goo
- 31. Snatch the Prize
- 32. Pressure Points
- 34. Body Hide
- 35. Snake Pit
- 36. Orkestra
- 38. The Audience: Yay! Boo!
- 40. The Provocateur
- 41. In and Out – But Only Two
- 42. Pop Goes the Beastie
- 43. The Invaders
- 44. Task and Time
- 45. The Eyes Have It: The Trick
- 46. The Variation
- 47. Incoming!
- 48. Object Leads
- 50. Properazzi
- 51. Prop Offers
- 52. Pass it Round
- 53. Embodied Image
- 54. Wind-Up, Stall, Repeat, Breathe
- 55. Pick a Mask
- 56. Physicalise a Phrase
- 57. Party Animals
- 60. The Benign Dictator
- 61. Shifty Solos
- 65. Cane Connection
- 66. Mirrors and Shadows
- 67. Dogged
- 69. Lookers
- 70. Be Seated
- 71. Three Coats, Three Hats and a Bench
- 73. Let Me Handle This
- 74. Disadvantaged
- 75. Tableaux
- 76. Machines and Slow-Motion Scenes
- 77. Repel and Lookout
- 78. The Journey
- 79. The Preposterous Players
- 80. The Escalating Party

Introductions
- 1. Name Games
- 2. Aura
- 4. Lean On Me
- 5. Human Springs
- 12. Alien, Cow, Lion
- 13. Mouse, Cat, Dog, Horse, Eagle
- 14. Clap It Round
- 48. Object Leads
- 65. Cane Connection

Leading
- 3. Hands to Hands
- 11. Let's Dance
- 19. Buf Da
- 32. Pressure Points
- 36. Orkestra
- 37. Who Started It?
- 43. The Invaders
- 50. Properazzi
- 51. Prop Offers
- 58. Segmented
- 66. Mirrors and Shadows
- 67. Dogged
- 68. The Solo Duet
- 69. Lookers
- 70. Be Seated
- 71. Three Coats, Three Hats and a Bench
- 73. Let Me Handle This
- 78. The Journey

Listening
- 4. Lean On Me
- 7. Awareness
- 8. Breath and Movement
- 9. Count Up, Count Down
- 12. Alien, Cow, Lion
- 16. Eyes Closed
- 17. You–Me
- 18. Game On
- 19. Buf Da
- 20. Wide-Eyed
- 23. Chain Reaction
- 26. The Eyes Have It: Choices
- 32. Pressure Points
- 35. Snake Pit
- 36. Orkestra
- 41. In and Out – But Only Two
- 46. The Variation
- 47. Incoming!
- 52. Pass it Round
- 58. Segmented
- 64. Walk Like Me
- 65. Cane Connection
- 66. Mirrors and Shadows

minimum-to-MAXIMUM
- 9. Count Up, Count Down
- 10. Ha-Ha-Ha! Wah-Wah-Wah…
- 42. Pop Goes the Beastie
- 54. Wind-Up, Stall, Repeat, Breathe
- 56. Physicalise a Phrase
- 57. Party Animals
- 63. Seven Snapshots
- 70. Be Seated
- 73. Let Me Handle This
- 80. The Escalating Party

Physical Expression
- 11. Let's Dance
- 21. Point of Focus
- 22. Takes
- 24. Entrances and Exits

25. The Audience: Hands
26. The Eyes Have It: Choices
38. The Audience: Yay! Boo!
39. Nice and Nasty
40. The Provocateur
45. The Eyes Have It: The Trick
46. The Variation
50. Properazzi
52. Pass it Round
53. Embodied Image
54. Wind-Up, Stall, Repeat, Breathe
55. Pick a Mask
56. Physicalise a Phrase
57. Party Animals
58. Segmented
59. The Set-Up and the Scene
60. The Benign Dictator
61. Shifty Solos
62. Solo Variations: Atmosphere
63. Seven Snapshots
64. Walk Like Me
68. The Solo Duet
69. Lookers
71. Three Coats, Three Hats and a Bench
75. Tableaux
76. Machines and Slow-Motion Scenes
80. The Escalating Party

Prop Play
47. Incoming!
48. Object Leads
49. Props-Go-Round
50. Properazzi
51. Prop Offers
57. Party Animals
58. Segmented
59. The Set-Up and the Scene
60. The Benign Dictator
61. Shifty Solos
62. Solo Variations: Atmosphere
63. Seven Snapshots
65. Cane Connection
67. Dogged
71. Three Coats, Three Hats and a Bench
72. Props, People, Status
74. Disadvantaged
78. The Journey
80. The Escalating Party

Solos
22. Takes
24. Entrances and Exits
26. The Eyes Have It: Choices
38. The Audience: Yay! Boo!
40. The Provocateur
45. The Eyes Have It: The Trick
46. The Variation
50. Properazzi
53. Embodied Image
55. Pick a Mask
58. Segmented
59. The Set-Up and the Scene
60. The Benign Dictator
61. Shifty Solos
62. Solo Variations: Atmosphere
63. Seven Snapshots

Status
42. Pop Goes the Beastie
43. The Invaders
66. Mirrors and Shadows
67. Dogged
69. Lookers
70. Be Seated
71. Three Coats, Three Hats and a Bench
72. Props, People, Status
73. Let Me Handle This

Timing
7. Awareness
8. Breath and Movement
13. Mouse, Cat, Dog, Horse, Eagle
14. Clap It Round
19. Buf Da
22. Takes
25. The Audience: Hands
26. The Eyes Have It: Choices
28. Fox and Squirrel
33. Dance and Get Off the Floor
35. Snake Pit
36. Orkestra
37. Who Started It?
43. The Invaders
44. Task and Time
45. The Eyes Have It: The Trick
47. Incoming!
51. Prop Offers
54. Wind-Up, Stall, Repeat, Breathe
62. Solo Variations: Atmosphere
68. The Solo Duet
69. Lookers
70. Be Seated
80. The Escalating Party

Trios
22. Takes
24. Entrances and Exits
30. Snatch Tail
31. Snatch the Prize
47. Incoming!
51. Prop Offers
69. Lookers
70. Be Seated
71. Three Coats, Three Hats and a Bench
72. Props, People, Status
73. Let Me Handle This
74. Disadvantaged

Trust
5. Human Springs
16. Eyes Closed
18. Game On
33. Dance and Get Off the Floor
43. The Invaders
64. Walk Like Me
74. Disadvantaged

Warm-Up
1. Name Games
3. Hands to Hands
4. Lean On Me
5. Human Springs
7. Awareness
8. Breath and Movement
9. Count Up, Count Down
11. Let's Dance
12. Alien, Cow, Lion
13. Mouse, Cat, Dog, Horse, Eagle
14. Clap It Round
15. Chase and Tag
16. Eyes Closed
17. You–Me
18. Game On
19. Buf Da
20. Wide-Eyed
21. Point of Focus
23. Chain Reaction
28. Fox and Squirrel
29. Dragon's Jewels

ALPHABETICAL LIST

12. Alien, Cow, Lion
25. The Audience: Hands
38. The Audience: Yay! Boo!
2. Aura
7. Awareness
70. Be Seated
60. The Benign Dictator
34. Body Hide
8. Breath and Movement
19. Buf Da
65. Cane Connection
23. Chain Reaction
15. Chase and Tag
14. Clap It Round
9. Count Up, Count Down
33. Dance and Get Off the Floor
74. Disadvantaged
67. Dogged
29. Dragon's Jewels
53. Embodied Image
24. Entrances and Exits
80. The Escalating Party
16. Eyes Closed
26. The Eyes Have It: Choices
45. The Eyes Have It: The Trick
28. Fox and Squirrel
18. Game On
27. Ha-goo
10. Ha-Ha-Ha! Wah-Wah-Wah…
3. Hands-to-Hands
5. Human Springs
41. In and Out – But Only Two
47. Incoming!
43. The Invaders
78. The Journey
6. Knot, Spiral, Pulse
4. Lean On Me
73. Let Me Handle This
11. Let's Dance
69. Lookers
76. Machines and Slow-Motion Scenes
66. Mirrors and Shadows
13. Mouse, Cat, Dog, Horse, Eagle
1. Name Games
39. Nice and Nasty
48. Object Leads
36. Orkestra
57. Party Animals
52. Pass It Round
56. Physicalise a Phrase
55. Pick a Mask
21. Point of Focus
42. Pop Goes the Beastie
79. The Preposterous Players
32. Pressure Points
51. Prop Offers
50. Properazzi
49. Props-Go-Round
72. Props, People, Status
40. The Provocateur
77. Repel and Lookout
58. Segmented
59. The Set-Up and the Scene
63. Seven Snapshots
61. Shifty Solos
35. Snake Pit
30. Snatch Tail
31. Snatch the Prize
68. Solo Duet
62. Solo Variations: Atmospheres
75. Tableaux
22. Takes
44. Task and Time
71. Three Coats, Three Hats and a Bench
46. The Variation
64. Walk Like Me
37. Who Started It?
20. Wide-Eyed
54. Wind-Up, Stall, Repeat, Breathe
17. You–Me

COMPLETE LIST

ALL GAMES PLUS VARIATIONS

1
Name Games
In-a-Circle Style
Mexican-Wave Name

2
Aura

3
Hands to Hands
Push Hands to Hands
Push Parts

4
Lean On Me
Back to Back
Body Part to Body Part
Touch Twister

5
Human Springs

6
Knot, Spiral, Pulse
Knot
Spiral
Pulse

7
Awareness
Start, Stop, Suspension
One Go
One Stop
Progression Start
Progression Stop

8
Breath and Movement
Breathe, Walk, Breathe
Breath Matches Movement

9
Count Up, Count Down
Warm-Up
The Count
Speed Count

10
Ha-Ha-Ha! Wah-Wah-Wah…
Warm-Up
Progression
Laughter to Tears

11
Let's Dance
Warm-Up
Isolations
Back-to-Back
Soul Train Line
Cool/Loony Dance
Body-Part Touching
Prop/Clothes Partner
Evocative
Tense/Loose Dance
Big Cheese
Obstacle-Course Disco

12
Alien, Cow, Lion

13
Mouse, Cat, Dog, Horse, Eagle
Test Run
Fast Chase
Mouse! Cat! Dog! Horse! Eagle!

14
Clap It Round
Clap, Raspberry, Oh!
Clap Together
Clap, Pass, Breathe

15
Chase and Tag
Heads and Tails, Hear It
Heads and Tails, See It
Hold-the-Chicken Tag
Hold-the-Chichen Tag Timed
Band-Aid Tag

16
Eyes Closed
Doo-Wee
Werewolf
Werewolf Freeze

17
You–Me
You–Me
You–Me Reverse

18
Game On

19
Buf Da
One Leader, One Ball
One Leader, Two Balls
Buf Da Chaos

20
Wide-Eyed

21
Point of Focus
Focus, Move, Stop
Energy Pull

22
Takes
Warm-Up
Solo Takes

23
Chain Reaction

24
Entrances and Exits

25
The Audience: Hands

26
The Eyes Have It: Choices
Never Look
Always Look
Choose Your Moment

27
Ha-goo

28
Fox and Squirrel

29
Dragon's Jewels

30
Snatch Tail
Duos
Trios
Slow-Mo

31
Snatch the Prize
Duos
Trios
Prize Held

32
Pressure Points
Ball, Palm, Body
The Derry Variation

33
Dance and Get Off the Floor

34
Body Hide
Four-Hiding-One
Hide-or-Be-Seen

35
Snake Pit

36
Orkestra
Circle Sounds
Rehearsal
Performance

37
Who Started It?

38
The Audience: Yay! Boo!

39
Nice and Nasty

40
The Provocateur
Say Yes
Yes, Tic, Wind-Up

41
In and Out – But Only Two
Only Two
Scene

42
Pop Goes the Beastie

43
The Invaders
In Your Space
Scene

44
Task and Time

45
The Eyes Have It: The Trick
Never Look
Always Look
Choose Your Moment

46
The Variation

47
Incoming!

48
Object Leads

49
Props-Go-Round

50
Properazzi

51
Prop Offers
Tag Team, Same Prop
Tag Team, New Prop, Same Scene
Tag Team, New Prop, New Scene

52
Pass It Round

53
Embodied Image

54
Wind-Up, Stall, Repeat, Breathe
Wind-Up
Stall
Repeat
Breathe

55
Pick a Mask

56
Physicalise a Phrase

57
Party Animals

58
Segmented

59
The Set-Up and the Scene

60
The Benign Dictator
One-Minute Act
Thirty-Second Act
Fifteen-Second Act
Two-Minute Act

61
Shifty Solos

62
Solo Variations: Atmospheres
With Reverence
Olympic Event
Teatro Grande

63
Seven Snapshots

64
Walk Like Me
Observers
Imitation
Guesswork

65
Cane Connection
Fingers–Cane–Fingers
Other Parts
Blind

66
Mirrors and Shadows
Mirror Me
Switches
Little Mirror
Wandering Mirrors
Shadow

67
Dogged

68
Solo Duet
My Mirror
Mirror Play

69
Lookers
Turn Away
Look Away

70
Be Seated

71
Three Coats, Three Hats and a Bench
Single Switch
Repeat

72
Props, People, Status
Player, Prop and Status
Change, Stay
Change, Move

73
Let Me Handle This

74
Disadvantaged
My Coat and Hat, Please
The Party

75
Tableaux
Types
Guess the Scene
Tableau Preparation

76
Machines and Slow-Motion Scenes

77
Repel and Lookout
Solo Repel
Group Repel
Lookout

78
The Journey

79
The Preposterous Players

80
The Escalating Party

www.nickhernbooks.co.uk

@nickhernbooks